SOTTERLEY
HER PEOPLE AND
THEIR WORLDS

SOTTERLEY
HER PEOPLE AND THEIR WORLDS

DAVID G. BROWN

Chesapeake
BOOK COMPANY

BALTIMORE, MARYLAND

2010

Library of Congress Cataloging-in-Publication Data

Brown, David G., 1940-
Sotterley : her people and their worlds / David G. Brown.
    p. cm.
Includes bibliographical references and index.
ISBN-13: 978-0-9823049-1-4 (alk. paper)
ISBN-10: 0-9823049-1-9 (alk. paper)
1. Sotterley Plantation (Md.) 2. Saint Mary's County (Md.)--
History, Local. 3. Saint Mary's County (Md.)--Biography. I. Title.

F187.S2B75 2010
975.2'41--dc22

                                        2009044414

Manufactured in the United States of America.
The paper used in this publication meets the minimum requirements
of the American National Standard for Information Sciences
Permanence of Paper for Printed Library Materials
ANSI Z39.48-1984.
Printed on recycled paper

Designed by James F. Brisson

*For all those who
love Sotterley*

CONTENTS

PREFACE AND ACKNOWLEDGMENTS

Sotterley, the only eighteenth-century tidewater plantation in Maryland that is now regularly open to the public, is located in a picturesque site overlooking the Patuxent River. Over the centuries it was occupied, those who lived there cleared land, raised crops, built homes, planted trees, tended gardens, and transformed the land into a charming estate that is attractive to the eye and soothing to the soul.

Sotterley is not the oldest home in Maryland or the grandest manor house on the Chesapeake, but it is a remarkably interesting architectural gem, with some of the best examples of colonial-era woodworking craftsmanship. Although the eighteenth- and nineteenth-century owners did not leave their own furnishings, Sotterley's collection includes museum quality furniture and other items. It never served as the home of an American president or a Civil War general or a famous scientist or poet. It is, however, a place where many people lived and worked, some prominent and others not, but a number of them interesting and all of whom contributed to Sotterley. Unfortunately some of their stories are unrecorded; those that were constitute the heart of this book. Together they have much to tell us about the history of St. Mary's County, the state of Maryland's early history, and by extension, that of the country. Sotterley is therefore a rich educational resource for understanding the origins of American culture.

Our understanding of Sotterley's long history is always deepening and expanding. What the Satterlees knew when they bought the property in 1910 differs from what Mabel Ingalls, the last owner, learned and what is still being discovered today. This book reflects our understanding in the summer of 2009. Over the years many tales have been told about Sotterley, some more imaginative than accurate. While not wanting to lose them, this book strives to be historically accurate. Although it is not encumbered by footnotes, sources used herein are located in Sotterley's archives and in the author's historical files there. Where primary sources were unavailable and where I am less certain of the information, I have qualified my statements with such phrases as "it appears" or "family accounts state."

Many people have preceded my research on Sotterley. Earlier work by Jeanette Fox Fausz, Agnes Kane Callum, Marylin Arrigan, and Kirk Ranzetta has been particularly useful. Sotterley's archives also contain many anonymous research notes. I am indebted to these known and unknown predecessors alike. Many from the Sotterley family also have contributed time and helpful comments, including Carolyn Hoey, Nancy Easterling, Marylin Arrigan, John O'Rourke, Pete Himmelheber, Stuart Fitrell and Pat Dunlap. Ruth Hill and Susan Furgeson at the St. Mary's County Historical Society have been immensely helpful with my research. Ralph Eshelman provided insights on the War of 1812 and introduced me to the research of the late Stanley Quick from which the account of Captain Brown's confrontation with John Plater is drawn. Professor Ken Cohen from St. Mary's College of Maryland provided comments on the eighteenth-century chapters and encouraged me to include a separate chapter on that period's slave community. Interviews conducted by volunteers working under the auspices of the Sotterley Oral History Project have provided much grist for twentieth-century chapters. John Hanson Briscoe, Agnes Kane Callum, Richard Knott, Sandra van Heerden, and Donald Barber have provided helpful suggestions on their families' stories. My daughter Christine has compensated for my lack of talent with graphics. My wife Erna's patience and support through this long project are deeply appreciated. I am indebted to all, for they have made this a better book. Any shortcomings or errors that remain are my own.

I am particularly grateful to Robert I. Cottom, my editor and publisher at the Chesapeake Book Company, for agreeing to take on this project. His thoughtful editing has greatly improved the text, and I've appreciated his expertise and patience in guiding me through the production process. My colleagues at Sotterley and I are indebted to Ric for his support and sense of public service.

Portions of the chapters on George Plater III are much abridged versions of articles previously published in the *Maryland Historical Magazine* and the *Chronicles of St. Mary's* and are reprinted here with permission. The full articles are listed in the section on additional reading. Images and graphics are from Sotterley unless otherwise noted.

This short book just scratches the surface of Sotterley's diverse people. Many details have been omitted, there is much more to be learned about those described in these pages, and more stories are there to be uncovered and told. Hopefully this book will encourage others to delve into their lives and enrich our understanding of Sotterley's people and their contributions to our common heritage.

Dave Brown
Shangri-la on Cuckold Creek
July 2009

Resurrection Manor. Courtesy, Patricia Heintzelman,
National Historic Landmark Program.

I

Past as Prelude

T HIS ACCOUNT OF Sotterley's people begins around 1700. Of course
that was not the beginning—Indians had been in the area, perhaps for a
millennium. When the English arrived early in the seventeenth century,
about 1,500 Indians were living in settled villages across southern Maryland,
in parts of what are now St. Mary's, Calvert, Charles and Prince George's
counties. They were a part of the Algonquin nation.

The Indians living along the river were known as the Patuxents, from
whom the English settlers took the name for the river. Captain John Smith's
map of his exploration of the Chesapeake Bay in 1608–9 indicates that there
were Indian villages along the Patuxent, though not in the area near Sotterley.
Archeology at Sotterley has produced many arrowheads but no evidence of an
Indian settlement. In contrast to experience elsewhere, relations between the
English settlers and the Indians in southern Maryland were quite friendly.
Although Maquacomen, the chief or weroance of the Patuxents, thought
highly of the English, particularly the Jesuit priests, by the 1650s disease
had reduced the number of Patuxents, and before the end of the seventeenth
century none remained in southern Maryland.

Thomas Cornwaleys (also spelled Cornwallis), one of Cecil Calvert,
second Lord Baltimore's commissioners, together with Calvert's brother
Leonard, arrived in Maryland in March 1634 aboard the *Ark* and the *Dove* to
begin the Maryland plantation. In 1650, Lord Baltimore granted a patent of

four thousand acres known as Resurrection Manor to Cornwaleys, land that included what is now Sotterley. Cornwaleys had his home at Cross Manor on St. Inigoes Creek, and there is no evidence that he ever lived on the additional acreage granted to him. Political troubles in early Maryland eventually led Thomas Cornwaleys to return to England.

The ownership of Resurrection Manor changed several times. In 1674, Captain Richard Perry purchased the property. It is probable that during his ownership, if not earlier, a modest brick manor house was built on what is now Scotch Point about five miles southwest of Sotterley. Although the manor house was designated a national historic landmark in 1970, its modern owners did not maintain it, and what was left of it was demolished in 2002 to make way for development. (This fate will not befall Sotterley.) In 1684, Edmund and George Plowden acquired Resurrection Manor from Captain Perry.

In addition to the owners, colonial records indicate that people, probably tenant farmers, lived on various parts of Resurrection Manor in the second half of the seventeenth century. There is a record of a mill on the stream leading into what is now Forest Landing Cove, so it is possible that at the end of the seventeenth century someone was living, legally or otherwise, on the land around Sotterley, but no records indicating who this might have been have survived.

2

Founding a Tidewater Tobacco Plantation

ABOUT 1699, James Bowles, son of prominent London sugar and tobacco merchant Tobias Bowles, arrived in Maryland. He came in part to settle the estate of a relative but also to establish a plantation that would supply tobacco to his father. Bowles was well educated, wealthy, related to John Seymour, who five years hence would become governor, and ambitious.

Just how and when Bowles became interested in what is now Sotterley is unclear. Around 1703 the first two-room house was erected there, probably by Bowles. A 1705 document mentions Bowles as being from the Patuxent River, and land records from 1710 indicate that he bought two thousand acres in Resurrection Manor from George Plowden, including what is now Sotterley. Colonial land sales were not always recorded promptly, and it is possible that Bowles was using the land before the purchase was recorded. Several years later in 1716, Bowles patented 890 acres from this purchase and named it "Bowles's Preservation." Over time other areas in his part of Resurrection Manor came to be known as "Masons," "Hogg Neck," "Scotch Neck," "Hectors," and "Half Pone." Together these constituted a potentially productive tobacco property. The Bowles house and other buildings were located near an inlet on the Patuxent that is now called Sotterley Creek, which provided easy access for ocean-going ships that could take tobacco to his father

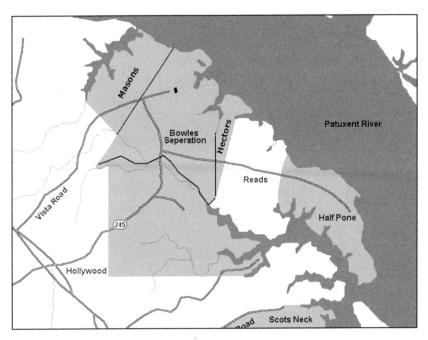

Land owned by James Bowles at his death in 1727.
Courtesy, Peter Himmelheber.

in London. Although we have no records of Bowles's tobacco production or exports, evidence suggests that the plantation prospered. In October 1709 the governor appointed Bowles as a justice of the peace in St. Mary's County, and in 1710 Bowles was elected to represent St. Mary's in the Lower House of the Assembly, indications that by then Bowles was a successful member of the county's land-owning elite. Around 1715, Bowles constructed a substantial addition to his original house that included a brick-lined cellar, closets on the first floor, and a full second-story bedroom with fireplace—all signs that the plantation could afford significant improvements. A dozen years later, the inventory of his estate provided additional evidence that the plantation was a successful enterprise. It mentioned among other things that he had a small library of about forty books and a cellar with wines and ciders, signs of a gentry family.

Tobacco was the cash crop that underpinned Bowles's wealth. In the early eighteenth century, planters in the Chesapeake tidewater raised tobacco with the aid of African slaves, and we know from the inventory of James Bowles's estate that he owned forty-one slaves when he died. Plantations were large because tobacco drained nutrients from the soil, and modern fertilizers were not available. Consequently, every six or seven years, after the soil in the working fields had been depleted, the tobacco crop had to be moved to newly cleared land. Only after twenty or twenty-five years of lying fallow could the fields be replanted in tobacco.

The crop was harvested in the fall and dried and packed over the winter in large barrels, called "hogsheads," for shipment to England the following year. Weighing up to a thousand pounds each, hogsheads were rolled down the "rolling road" to a planter's dock.

Bowles's wharf was on Sotterley Creek. The ships that called on Sotterley may have arrived directly from England laden with goods Bowles had ordered from London because they could not be produced on the plantation. It is also possible that ships arrived as part of what was known as the triangular trade, wherein products from England were first carried to Africa for sale in exchange for slaves, the slaves were shipped to the Caribbean or the British colonies in North America for resale, and the tobacco and a few other exports from the colonies were exported to England. Whatever the case, Sotterley was involved in a thriving international trade from the time of its founding. James Bowles and his father were in a position to profit from such trade by exporting tobacco and importing slaves or servants for resale. Surviving records show that in 1720 Bowles placed an order for 270 slaves, far more than he needed on his plantation, from the Royal African Company. Although there is no record to confirm that these slaves were received, it seems clear that Bowles intended to participate in the slave trade. He also shipped corn and livestock—beyond that which he needed for Sotterley—to other plantations on the Chesapeake and to other colonies via the coastal trade.

Bowles's social connections brought him political reward and a respectable family life. In 1720 he was appointed to the Governor's Council, the influential group of men who advised the governor on public matters and who also served as the Upper House of the General Assembly. Bowles retained this position until his death. In 1718 he married Jane Lowe, who died shortly after delivering their daughter, Jane Lowe Bowles. A few years later, James Bowles married Rebecca Addison, daughter of the politically prominent Thomas Addison and the very wealthy Elizabeth Tasker Addison. James and Rebecca had two daughters, Eleanor and Mary.

By the time he died in 1727, "Bowles Preservation" was like many other tidewater plantations. It was a small community comprising the Bowles family, their forty-one slaves, and undoubtedly a few white overseers to manage the enslaved Africans. The plantation was typical of the other plantations around Chesapeake Bay, and its roughly fifty inhabitants constituted about one percent of the population of St. Mary's County.

Bowles's will left the plantation to his three daughters. While Jane, his oldest daughter by his first marriage, received title to the area surrounding the main house, James granted Rebecca a life interest in the property that included use of the house. His will stated, "my desire is my children may all live in love and amity and be dutiful to their mother, and that their mother will be loving and tender to them." If this hinted at any friction among the children, there is no other indication to support the notion. Faced with the responsibilities of a young family and a large plantation, it is hardly surprising that Rebecca considered a new marriage. Her family connections and the wealth of the plantation made her an eligible widow, but she demonstrated no urgency in finding another husband.

The Original House

THE ORIGINAL HOUSE at Sotterley was built about 1703. It was a simple two-room structure of earth-fast or post-in-ground construction. Cyprus and cedar logs were trimmed and placed upright in holes about three feet deep to serve as a frame for the house. The building measured approximately twenty-two by forty-five feet and had brick chimneys at its northern and southern ends. Above the two rooms was a loft. There was probably a separate kitchen building, but no trace of such a structure has been found.

Rough clapboard siding and wooden shingles on the roof probably covered the exterior of the building. The interior was plastered and then white-washed. This was a simple, functional house, distinguished from others only by virtue of having two rooms rather than one. Just how the rooms were used is uncertain. Possibly the larger, northern room served as the main hall and the smaller southern room was Madame Bowles's chamber. Few post-in-ground houses from the period survive. At Sotterley, the southern room of the first house remains in its original place and shape, and the original pillars placed in the ground over three hundred years ago are intact.

Parts of the original structure survived because successive owners renovated rather than replaced the buildings they inherited. James Bowles started this process when he added a "new room" on the west of the original house around 1715.

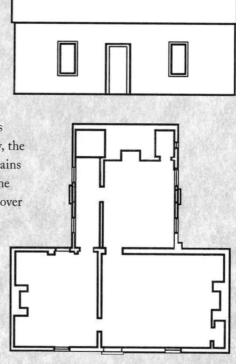

The front of the Bowles house (above), and its floor plan.

George Plater II.

3

Prosperity and Expansion

I n June 1729, Rebecca Bowles married George Plater II. Her new husband was the son of George Plater I, who had emigrated to Maryland in the late seventeenth century and risen to be attorney general in the colonial administration. His mother was Ann Doyne. Although his father died when he was only twelve, George Plater II managed to acquire an excellent legal education at the Inns of Court in London and returned to Maryland to pursue a career as a lawyer in the county and provincial courts. In 1727 he was appointed clerk to the Governor's Council, and in 1729 a justice in the Provincial Court.

It is not surprising that George and Rebecca met, for they were both members of prominent Maryland families. Rebecca was a wealthy widow, George a thirty-five-year-old bachelor, which was unusual in the eighteenth century. (Our story will show that it was fortunate he was available when Rebecca was looking for a new husband.) The *Maryland Gazette* of June 17, 1729, carried the brief announcement that "George Plater Esq. was married to Mrs. Rebecca Bowles, the relict [widow] of James Bowles Esq., a gentlewoman of considerable fortune."

Plater owned a house in Annapolis, where he conducted his legal work, but it is unclear how he and Rebecca divided their time between Annapolis and Sotterley in the early years of their marriage. Some of their children were said to have been born in Annapolis. Yet, it seems certain that over time the large plantation held by his wife became his principal residence. Together they raised a small family of their own, developed a prosperous plantation, and expanded and improved their house.

Land and government positions were two major sources of wealth in colonial Maryland, and George Plater II had both, as well as income from his legal profession. In the year of his marriage, he was appointed to the lucrative official position of Naval Officer of the Patuxent, a customs position, charged with clearing ships into and out of the Patuxent River and collecting duties on the export of tobacco. The income from this office alone would have been sufficient to support a gentleman in comfort. In 1732 he, like James Bowles before him, received an appointment to the Governor's Council and Upper House of the Assembly. A final mark of high standing was bestowed just before his unexpected death, when he was appointed secretary of the province, one of the governor's most prestigious, influential, and best remunerated positions.

By the time of his death in 1755, George Plater II had become one of the largest landowners in Maryland. Rebecca had died sometime around 1742, and George had gradually begun buying the various pieces of James Bowles's holdings from Rebecca's three daughters, who had all married men living in Virginia. In addition, he acquired most of the rest of Resurrection Manor and other land lying to the south toward Town Creek, giving him ownership of more than seven thousand acres in St. Mary's County adjacent to Sotterley. Plater also owned approximately seven thousand more acres in Prince George's, Montgomery, Caroline, and other Maryland counties. The Tobacco Inspection Law, adopted in 1747, favored large planters who could produce high quality tobacco, and contributed to the profitability and expansion of Plater's tobacco business.

George and Rebecca had raised three children of their own—two daughters, Rebecca and Elizabeth, and a son, George. Together they arranged for the marriages of Rebecca's three daughters by her previous marriages to prominent families in Virginia. After his wife's death, George saw their daughter, Rebecca, marry James Tayloe of Mt. Airy, also in Virginia. These advantageous marriages expanded the family's relationships with other prominent Chesapeake families.

George and Rebecca's extensive holdings of land and slaves, their family connections, and his education made them members of the small gentry elite

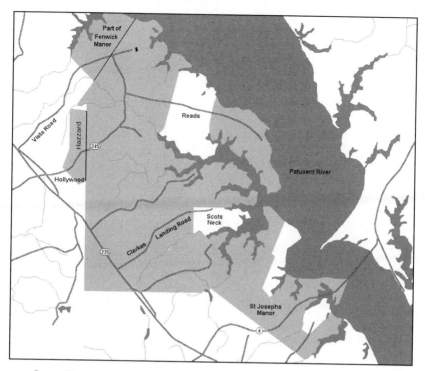

George Plater II's land adjoining Sotterley in 1755. Courtesy, Peter Himmelheber.

that dominated Chesapeake society. In the middle of the eighteenth century, these families comprised about 7 percent of Maryland's population. A thousand acres could produce the income needed to live as a "gentleman," and since Plater owned about fourteen thousand acres, his family was among the elite. Below the gentry in the social and economic order, other planter families with well more than the fifty acres required to vote constituted another 16 percent of the population. Beneath them were small landowners, poor tenant farmers, and white indentured servant families, altogether forming about 48 percent. At the lowest rung of society were black slaves and a few free blacks who made up the remaining 29 percent.

No records survive to indicate how many slaves George Plater II owned at Sotterley, his home in Annapolis, or on his other properties, though it is likely that the number at Sotterley alone was around one hundred. The plantation's prosperity made it possible for George and Rebecca to expand and improve the main house at Sotterley. A few years after their marriage, they added a large addition on the southern end, and later they began the laborious process of putting wood paneling on three rooms that James Bowles had built. Skilled slave workers undoubtedly performed much of the work. On Plater's death in 1755, his only son George inherited all of his land and slaves.

Five George Platers

THE PLATER FAMILY from Suffolk, England, included five generations of George Platers in Maryland, four of whom owned Sotterley over the course of almost one hundred years. None of the five had a middle name to help us differentiate one from another, and the second George did not use "Jr." after his name. The third was a colonel in the provincial militia and was at the time often referred to as "Colonel Plater." To add to the confusion, his father and son were also militia colonels.

As a convenience, this book refers to them as George Plater I, George Plater II and so on. For the record their lives spanned the following years: George Plater I (c.1664–1705), George Plater II (1695–1755), George Plater III (1735–1792), George Plater IV (1766–1802) and George Plater V (1796–1846)

The first George Plater, spelled Playter, was a member of a branch of the Playter family that then owned Sotterley Hall in Suffolk, England. Educated at Cambridge and having studied law in the offices of an attorney, he is believed to have sailed from England about 1688 with a sizeable fortune, £3,000, to begin a new life in Maryland. He arrived in St. Mary's amidst the turmoil of the Glorious Revolution, and in 1689 he signed the Address of Protestant Inhabitants of St. Mary's County, a statement of support for William and Mary. His son George Plater II reportedly changed the spelling of the family name.

Ports of Entry and
Tobacco Inspection

For CUSTOMS PURPOSES, eighteenth-century colonial Maryland was divided into "ports of entry," each of which was headed by a naval officer, whose job it was to collect fees on the entry and departure of ships and to levy duties on the export of tobacco. Some of these ports were in towns such as Annapolis or Oxford; others were in areas such as the Patuxent or Potomac. On entering a river, the captain of an incoming ship had to determine where the naval officer or his designee conducted official business. At different times during the eighteenth century, George Plater II and George Plater III served as Naval Officer for the Patuxent, which meant that incoming and outgoing ships had to stop near Sotterley Creek to complete their official paperwork.

In 1747, Maryland instituted a tobacco inspection regime to maintain standards for the quality of the tobacco the colony produced. The system required that tobacco be sent to designated inspection warehouses. Sotterley was never selected as the location for an inspection warehouse, in part because members of the Assembly could not serve as inspectors. The closest inspection warehouses to Sotterley were located to the north at Cole's Creek or to the south on Hugh Hopewell's land near Town Creek.

The "1757" Brick Warehouse

Sotterley's Brick Warehouse. Photo by David Brown.

THE DATE 1757 is built into the brickwork of an old building at Sotterley. The earliest written reference to a brick building there is on a tax list from 1798, but it is quite possible that it was built as early as 1757. What the building was used for is also not clear. The 1798 list refers to a brick stable. Although records at the time do not mention a warehouse, the building might have been used at some point to store hogsheads or other items ready for shipping. Subsequently the building was enlarged and a wooden shed added on the south side. In the twentieth century the building was known as the "customs warehouse," though this name was not mentioned in any eighteenth-century records.

4

Success in Colonial Maryland

GEORGE PLATER III was born on November 8, 1735, at Sotterley, the second child and only son of George and Rebecca Plater. Little is known of his early life. It appears that he was educated at home, as was customary. During 1753 and 1754, George was enrolled as a student at the College of William and Mary in Williamsburg, Virginia, where he would have taken a general course in Latin, religion, and science. Education at William and Mary was for the elite, and college records indicate that the young Plater was one of only a few students who was accompanied at school by a "boy," a black slave who looked after his horse and other needs.

In 1755, shortly after George finished at William and Mary, his father died, during what had become a tumultuous time in the colonies. The Seven Years' War, or French and Indian War, had erupted as Great Britain and France contested ownership of the vast lands west of the Appalachians. That summer, General Edward Braddock's army of British regulars and colonial militia suffered a stunning defeat that spread panic across western Maryland. Further study was no longer a choice George had the freedom to pursue.

At nineteen he inherited Sotterley, his father's other land and slaves, and his economic and social responsibilities as a member of Maryland's gentry. In April 1757, he was elected a warden of All Faith Parish where his family worshiped. In eighteenth-century Maryland, vestrymen and wardens were seen as responsible not just for church affairs but for certain economic and social issues in the parish. The warden and vestry positions, along with delegates to the Lower House of the Assembly, were the only elected offices in colonial Maryland, and vestry service was a sign that one had attained respect and position in local society. Later that year, Plater was appointed a judge of the St. Mary's County Court, often a step toward higher and more financially rewarding offices. That same year, he was elected to be one of St. Mary's County's four delegates to the Lower House of the Maryland Assembly.

Members of the Lower House divided themselves into two parties. The Proprietary Party, as its name implied, generally supported the interests of the Proprietor, Lord Baltimore, and cooperated with his representative, who at that time was Governor Horatio Sharpe. The Popular Party generally opposed the Proprietor's financial interests and defended the rights given Maryland citizens under the colonial charter. Coming from a family that had long benefited from association with the Calvert family, Plater not surprisingly cooperated with the Proprietary Party, and throughout his nearly ten years in the Lower House, he was a reliable supporter of the Proprietor.

Sometime in late 1759, George Plater departed on his first, and only, trip to England and returned to Maryland around June 1761. Just what Plater did in London is not entirely clear, though tobacco and his business interests were probably important reasons for his trip. Two of his contemporaries, Edmund Key and Charles Carroll, barrister, were in England at the same time studying law and were admitted to the Inns of Court, where George's father had been educated, but there is no record that Plater pursued a legal education. Whether he visited Sotterley Hall in Suffolk, which had by then been sold to the Barnes family, is also uncertain.

What George did do was call on Lord Baltimore's secretary, Cecilius Calvert, and ask for a position in the colonial administration. According to Calvert, Plater also met Frederick Calvert, the sixth Lord Baltimore, and made a favorable impression on him. But whether he was to get a position after his return to Maryland would also depend on Governor Horatio Sharpe, whose correspondence gives us the earliest assessment of Plater. In 1761, Sharpe wrote, "I have a very good opinion of his disposition and was well satisfied with his conduct during the session or two he appeared in the Lower House yet he is not thought a person of extraordinary abilities and is very young being I suppose scarcely 24 years old." Plater was re-elected to the Lower House in 1761 and continued to serve until 1767.

In 1762, Plater married Hannah Lee, who unfortunately died during childbirth about ten months later. In 1764 he was married again, this time to Elizabeth Rousby. Both marriages strengthened his connections with important Maryland families. Hannah's father, Richard Lee, was a member of the council and later president of the Upper House of the Assembly from 1772 to 1776. The Rousbys were a prominent family from Calvert County across the Patuxent. Elizabeth's stepfather was William Fitzhugh, who became one of the closest friends of Robert Eden, the last British governor of Maryland. Between 1765 and 1772, the Platers had two daughters and three sons who survived.

George Plater III as a young man.
From J. Thomas Scharf,
History of Maryland.

Although very little information on Plater's tobacco business has been found, it appears that he prospered during the 1760s and early 1770s. The remarkable rise in the demand for tobacco in the decades before the American Revolution generally brought wealth to larger planters. Plater also acted as his own factor, arranging to ship his tobacco to firms in London. In the 1770s he dealt with James Russell of Coutts & Co., exporting his tobacco and ordering goods in return. He also made purchases through James Glassford & Co., a firm with extensive commercial connections to the Chesapeake Bay plantations.

It was in these years that the Platers expanded and transformed their home at Sotterley into an elegant residence. Around 1761, George decided to raise the front roof of the mansion into a shed dormer that created additional bedrooms. About 1770, he and Elizabeth decided to expand the house toward the north, creating space for an entry hall and an elegant drawing room for entertaining. Richard Boulton, a master carpenter and joiner who had designed and built churches in the county, is credited with the design of this project, including Sotterley's Chinese Chippendale banister in the entry hall and the shell alcoves and other charming features of the new drawing room. Undoubtedly, slaves owned by Plater provided most of the skilled and unskilled labor for the creation of these beautiful rooms.

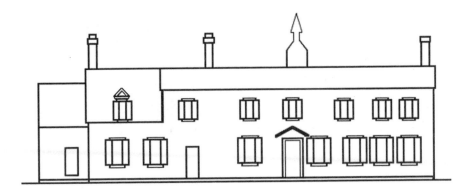

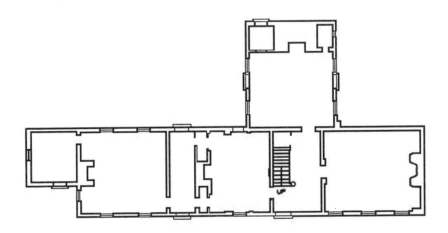

Front view of the Plater house.(above) and its floor plan.

It is still uncertain whether it was George II or George III who began to call this home Sotterley, after Sotterley Hall in Suffolk, the Plater family's ancestral home. The earliest contemporary mention of the name Sotterley is in a letter George III wrote in 1776. No use of the name in George II's time has been found.

In the 1760s, George Plater played a leading role in establishing the new St. Andrews Parish. The parish was created by taking territory from two existing Anglican parishes, one of which was All Faith, where Plater had been serving on the vestry. After Reverend Urquhart of All Faith passed away in 1764, planning for a church for St. Andrew's Parish could begin. That year, Plater was elected a vestryman at St. Andrews, and in 1765 he presented a bill in the Lower House to build a church for St. Andrew's. The bill authorized the purchase of two acres and imposed a levy on the citizens of the parish of 200,000 pounds of tobacco to pay for construction. In 1766, St. Andrew's vestry, in which Plater continued to be a member, decided to build the new church based on a design created by Richard Boulton. In 1769, after the church was completed, Plater and Abraham Barnes purchased pew number one, the most prestigious and expensive pew in the new church, for £16, a gesture that reflected Plater's leadership in his community and his life-long support for the Anglican Church.

George Plater's consistent support of the Proprietor's interest was eventually rewarded. In 1767, Sharpe appointed him Naval Officer of the Patuxent. As Naval Officer, Plater was no longer eligible to serve in the Lower House, for he now held an official position within the governor's administration, one that brought with it a substantial income of about £130 a year. Plater apparently fulfilled his new responsibilities satisfactorily, because a year later, as he himself was being replaced, Governor Sharpe wrote that if the position were to become vacant "I do not think it could be more properly conferred."

Just how Plater's relationship with the next and last royal governor, Robert Eden, developed has not yet come to light. Eden was generally popular among the landed gentry, and apparently he regarded Plater highly, because in 1771 he appointed the "Honorable Colonel George Plater" a member of "his Lordships Council of State," more commonly known as the governor's council. With this appointment, Plater became a member of the inner circle of men who ran the province. Unfortunately, his timing was not the best. Four years later the colonies were at war with Great Britain.

George Plater III.

5

A Revolutionary Patriot

Long-brewing tensions with Britain flared up after Parliament imposed a tax on tea in 1773, and erupted in open warfare at Lexington and Concord, Massachusetts, in April 1775. During these years, George Plater was a member of Governor Robert Eden's council. As the council records for those years have been lost, it is not clear what if any advice Plater offered.

Letters he wrote in this period do make clear that his sympathies lay with the colonial cause. In January 1775, Plater wrote to his business representative in London, James Russell, expressing his view that "the Americans" have "just rights" that they will never allow to be transgressed and warning that if Great Britain persisted in its policy, it would lead to the destruction of both Britain and the colonies. It was his hope that Parliament would make some gesture toward reconciliation. Clearly, Plater believed in the justice of the colonies' cause well before he was prepared to act in support of it.

Citizens in Maryland were already organizing to resist British policy. The first Maryland Convention, unauthorized by the governor, met in June 1774 and chose delegates for the first Continental Congress, which met in Philadelphia that September. Plater played no role in these early actions. In August 1775, when ardent patriots got the Maryland Convention to demand that all citizens sign an "Association of the Freemen of Maryland," declaring themselves in support of the patriot cause, Plater's name was not on the initial list of "Associators." In his report to London on these events, Governor Eden mentioned those in his administration who had gone over to the convention but made no mention of Plater.

The following month, citizens in St. Mary's County elected Plater one of their representatives to the next session of the Maryland Convention. Presumably, the voters had some reason to believe or hope that Plater's loyalties were changing, but Plater did not attend that session of the convention.

A few months later in February 1776, Plater was asked to raise money for the colonial cause, and he agreed to do so. Shortly thereafter, he was chosen to represent Maryland in talks with counterparts in Virginia in a plan to create a network of beacons along the Potomac River to warn of British naval movements. This too he did. Perhaps as early as late 1775, and certainly by February 1776, Plater had chosen to throw his support behind the patriot cause.

In May 1776, Plater was elected to the seventh Maryland Convention. This time, he took his seat and continued to serve in the ensuing sessions. The seventh convention met shortly after Samuel Purviance had launched a misguided attempt to capture Governor Eden, an episode that raised the politically sensitive issue of Eden's status. On one hand, Eden remained remarkably popular with Maryland leaders, and he had used his influence to finesse controversial issues that had led to conflict in other colonies. But John Hancock then president of the Continental Congress, had called on Maryland to arrest him. Plater led the convention's consideration of how to handle Eden and helped craft a moderate, pragmatic solution that permitted the governor a safe and graceful departure. Plater then helped prepare and deliver the message informing Eden he must leave. The message conveyed the convention's respect and its hope that when Eden returned to London he would work for reconciliation on terms acceptable to the colonies. A decade later, when Eden returned to Maryland as a private citizen, he visited the Platers at Sotterley. Their friendship had survived the war.

As late as May 1776 the patriot leadership in Maryland still hoped for an acceptable reconciliation with Britain. The convention had in fact just reiterated its instructions to its delegates in Philadelphia that they must not agree to independence without further authorization from Annapolis. But support for independence was developing rapidly in other colonies. After Patrick Henry moved his famous resolution that these colonies "are, and of right ought to be, free and independent states," the Continental Congress asked Maryland and other undecided colonies to reconsider independence.

A new Maryland convention met in late June with Plater again attending.

The decisive vote regarding independence came on a motion of whether votes in the convention should continue to be by county or whether individual delegate's votes should be counted. Voting by county favored the loyalist Eastern Shore. In a close vote, St. Mary's delegates, including Plater, joined the majority in deciding to switch to voting by delegate. Then on June 28, Plater joined in a unanimous decision by those delegates remaining at the convention to support independence. Four days later, the Continental Congress made its fateful decision. Plater had effectively committed himself to the Declaration's famous language: "We mutually pledge to each other our Lives, our Fortunes and our sacred Honor."

No letters explaining Plater's support for the patriot cause or his decision for independence have been found, yet these were remarkable decisions for a man whose family had served the colonial administration for three generations. Of the twelve men on the governor's council, only George Plater and Daniel of St. Thomas Jenifer supported the decision for independence.

At the end of the seventh convention in May, Plater was chosen for the first time to be a member of the Council of Safety. This was a rudimentary executive organ charged with implementing the convention's policies between sessions, and it meant that Plater was involved in implementing Maryland's preparations for war until the new state government was formed in late 1776. In November 1776, Plater was elected to the new Maryland Senate, and in November 1777 he was chosen as one of Maryland's delegates to the Continental Congress. For the three years of his service in the Congress, he had to shuttle back and forth between Philadelphia and his Senate responsibilities in Annapolis. For almost seven years, from May 1776 until the Peace of Paris took effect in the spring of 1783, Plater was actively involved in prosecuting the war and supporting the patriot cause. Among the myriad issues in which he was involved, a few help illustrate his character and role in the war.

In the fall of 1776, George Plater was part of a majority in the last Maryland Convention when it voted to abolish the poll tax in Maryland— a levy that fell equally on all freemen regardless of their economic circumstances—and to fund the new state government by taxes based on a person's ability to pay. Wealthy families such as his own would shoulder the tax burden. Several months later, as a senator in the new Maryland General Assembly, Plater voted for the Legal Tender Bill, which provided that existing debts denominated in pounds sterling could be repaid with rapidly depreciating paper money. Again, this measure ran counter to the interests of wealthy men like Plater who had lent funds in sterling. Both measures, though controversial, were perceived to be important in winning support for the new state government and the patriot cause. The political influence of ordinary freemen in government affairs was limited, but now government was adopting economic measures favorable to them. In voting for these laws, Plater and other gentry leaders placed the patriot cause ahead of their financial interest.

In 1777, Congress adopted the Articles of Confederation as a means of binding the new states together. As a senator, Plater had supported Maryland's view that vast western lands should be controlled by the new confederation rather than remaining the territory of those states whose western boundaries extended to the Mississippi River. Having no western lands of its own, Maryland would benefit if control was shifted to the central government. Besides, many prominent Maryland leaders, though not Plater, had speculated in land in the Ohio Valley. When Maryland's position was rejected, the Maryland Assembly voted not to ratify the Articles until the provisions regarding western lands were changed.

Although Plater had originally supported Maryland's position in the Senate and represented it at the Congress in Philadelphia, he gradually changed his mind. By late 1778 he was urging ratification. By 1780, Maryland was the only state that still had not ratified the Articles. Then two things happened. First, New York and Virginia indicated a willingness to relinquish their western lands. A short time later, British armies moved north into Virginia, and France, whose aid was essential, threatened to withhold military assistance if the states did not demonstrate their unity by adopting the Articles. In this atmosphere, the Maryland Senate reconsidered ratification in January 1781. At that moment, Plater was elected president of the Senate and immediately arranged a new vote in which the Articles were approved. Although Maryland's position on western lands had not been firmly secured, Plater had tried to ensure that the states would continue to act in common purpose.

In 1779, Plater had participated in the Continental Congress's consideration of the terms for peace with Britain. He joined the majority of delegates in requiring Britain to acknowledge the states' independence, to withdraw all its troops, and to accept the boundaries of the United States. Plater also supported a compromise that would have had the negotiators seek recognition of the New England states' fishing rights but not make this a necessary requirement for peace.

A year later, the heady days when the Continental Congress declared independence had long since past. Facing the government were the difficult tasks of finding supplies for Washington's army, raising funds to continue the war, fighting inflation, and navigating the dangerous shoals of appointments to office and investigations of misconduct therein. Service in Congress became less an honor and more of a burden. The Articles of Confederation limited delegates to three consecutive years in Congress, but few served that long. Plater was one of only a handful who served for three years until he left Philadelphia for the last time in December 1780.

He returned just as British troops under Cornwallis moved north into Virginia, from whence they threatened Maryland, and it was at that moment that Plater secured Maryland's support for the Articles of Confederation. For the remainder of the war until the Peace of Paris in 1783, Plater was with few interruptions the president of the Senate and consumed with the issues of war and peace.

With Plater's wealth and his role in the revolution came danger. In 1780 the British burned Rousby Hall, Elizabeth's childhood home, across the Patuxent. William Fitzhugh, her stepfather, was visiting Sotterley at the time, and it was feared Sotterley too might be attacked. On a few occasions the Platers were forced to abandon Sotterley to avoid similar depredations. In February 1782 a band of brigands led by Joseph Wheland raided Sotterley and absconded with several of Plater's slaves. Such criminal activities were a sign of the still chaotic social conditions. In March 1783, before word that the Treaty of Paris had been signed reached Maryland, British forces raided Sotterley. Plater wrote Gouverneur Morris that "I am again driven from my home by the Enemy's Barges, being obliged to have everything moved away, when they came and hung my Overseer, and the same fate I should probably have met had I been there."

The war disrupted the tobacco trade and threatened the livelihood of Maryland planters. Records of Plater's business during the war have not been found, and it is uncertain to what extent he shifted some land from tobacco into growing wheat, for which there was strong demand. His letters reflect concern with the effects of inflation and poor economic conditions. The war tempted other men into profiteering, but no such charges were ever made against him. At the war's end, Plater had preserved all the land that was his most important asset.

Elizabeth Rousby Plater.

6

Elizabeth Rousby Plater

Elizabeth Rousby Plater was the daughter of Anne Frisby and her first husband, John Rousby III. Although the date of her birth is not known, it appears she was born in late 1750 at Rousby Hall. The Rousbys, a wealthy family in Calvert County, had long been active in the colonial administration of Maryland. John Rousby died in January 1751, and about a year later, Anne agreed to marry Colonel William Fitzhugh, a prominent Virginian, who moved into Rousby Hall.

Elizabeth married George Plater III on July 19, 1764, when she was merely thirteen years old and sixteen years younger than her husband. That some women married at a very young age was not unusual for the time. The first of their children, Rebecca, was born just over a year later. Between then and 1774, Elizabeth had four more children who survived: George, John Rousby, Thomas, and Ann. According to family history recorded by her great-granddaughter in 1881, Elizabeth was a woman of great beauty and style, proud, and stern of demeanor.

Despite her early marriage and motherhood, Elizabeth somehow acquired an education. It is probable, as was often the case among the gentry, that she was educated at home by her parents or a tutor. She certainly had her mother Anne to thank for her social graces, which were often noted at the time, but beyond the social arts she also learned to read and write. That qualified her as a "gentlewoman." She apparently preferred to be called Eliza, a common nickname for Elizabeth, for that was how she signed her correspondence.

While George Plater III was serving in the Continental Congress from 1778 to 1780, Elizabeth was one of the few wives to accompanied their husbands to Philadelphia. James Lovell, another delegate to the Congress, wrote in October 1780 that, "She submits to the trouble of lodging up two pair of stairs rather than not be in Philadelphia with her husband." As a young woman of twenty-eight, it is not surprising that she attracted attention or that flattering comments regarding her beauty, culture, and fashion appeared in letters written by congressional delegates and foreign dignitaries. For example, the Marquis of Chastellux was a major general and deputy commander of the French expeditionary force that helped Washington win the decisive battle at Yorktown. On meeting Elizabeth in Philadelphia he recorded in his diary, "Should any stern philosopher be disposed to censure French manners, I would not advise him to do so in the presence of Mrs. P. [Plater], whom I waited upon after leaving Mrs. Bache. She is typical of Philadelphia's charming women; her taste is as delicate as her health; an enthusiast to excess for all French fashion, she is only waiting for the end of this little revolution to effect a still greater one in the manners of her country."

The Marquis was not the only prominent man Elizabeth captivated with her charms. Gouverneur Morris, a prosperous businessman representing New York in the Continental Congress, met the Platers in Philadelphia. Morris was a young bachelor and ladies' man a year younger than Eliza. They met in 1778, and he was much taken by her. On a carriage ride with the Platers in May 1780, an accident occurred in which Morris's leg was so severely injured that it had to be amputated. The Platers offered him lodging in their rooms while he recovered, and Eliza nursed him until they returned to Maryland at the end of May. In that short time he appears to have fallen in love with her. For many years afterward, he maintained a correspondence with the couple. To what extent she returned his romantic feelings is not clear, but her own feelings for him may well have been strong. "You say you wish much to see me," she wrote in a letter to Morris in 1782. "This wish is in your own power, but I will say no more on this subject lest I should go too far, as I have once or twice done, only be assured that nothing would give me so much pleasure." Just what Eliza meant is uncertain, but it did not affect her marriage, for there is ample evidence of continuing familial affection. Nevertheless, the impression her beauty and character had made on Morris was lasting. He was in London in 1790 when he learned that she had died, and he confessed in his diary: "I get away as soon as possible that I may not discover emotions which I cannot conceal. Poor Eliza! My lovely friend; thou art at peace and I shall behold thee no more. Never, never, never."

From about 1779 on, Elizabeth suffered recurrent health problems, but her discomfort did not prevent her from accompanying George to Annapolis and the Maryland Senate or keep her from an active social life. Family stories recount that her two daughters, Rebecca and Ann, were both as remarkably attractive as she was. Elizabeth and Rebecca, then nineteen, were in Annapolis in December 1783 when George Washington gave up his commission as commander-in-chief, and they danced at the ball given in Washington's honor. Six months later, in July 1784, former British governor Robert Eden visited Colonel Plater and his family at Sotterley. He fell ill while there and wrote a friend that he was being "tenderly nursed by the Colonel's family." Two months later Eden passed away in Annapolis. In September 1788 the Platers with their two daughters visited George and Martha Washington at Mount Vernon.

On October 11, 1789, Rebecca married General Uriah Forrest, a hero of the American Revolution. Family stories indicate that Elizabeth was at first opposed to her daughter marrying an older man who had lost a leg at the battle of Germantown but that she relented upon seeing their love for one another. Unfortunately, she did not live to see her other daughter or her sons marry. She died at Sotterley a few weeks later at the age of thirty-nine.

The bannister in the entry hall.

7

Richard Boulton:
Master Carpenter

Richard Boulton was a skilled carpenter and joiner who worked in St. Mary's County in the second half of the eighteenth century. He is believed to have been born in England, and there has been speculation that he had gotten into trouble with the law and been shipped along with other convicts to the colonies as an indentured servant. This may be true, but there is no record to substantiate it. Boulton first appeared in the records with a contract in 1761 to perform work on St. Thomas Manor for the Jesuit George Hunter. His contract stipulated that he was to be given "five shillings a day, a bottle of rum a week, and not condemn him to eat homini at his meal." It seems he had penchant for liquor, which may have been behind the story that he had gotten in trouble in England. In any event, he did not like hominy, a traditional Indian food made by soaking dried corn kernels until they were edible.

In 1766, St. Andrew's Parish, where George Plater III was a leading vestryman, was planning the construction of its first church. Boulton presented a design for which he was paid £5. Although other men did the construction work, the current St. Andrew's Church is based on Boulton's design. That same year, Boulton and Samuel Abell Jr. were given the contract to build a new church for All Faith Parish in Mechanicsville. All Faith's new church was completed in December 1767. Both churches survive as tributes to his craftsmanship.

According to records, Boulton was overseeing additional work on St. Andrew's Church in March 1770. Probably about that time, he is credited with creating the design for the expansion of nearby Sotterley that created a new entry hall and drawing room. Trained in England, Boulton would have been aware of the work of Thomas Chippendale, which evidently provided the inspiration for his design of the unique and beautiful Chinese Chippendale banister in Sotterley's entry hall. It seems probable that Boulton also designed and supervised the construction of the shell alcoves and other delicate features of the new drawing room. Although Boulton probably did the fine carpentry work himself, skilled slaves probably did much of the work on the entry hall and drawing room.

The alcoves in the drawing room.

Boulton's most important employer might have been George Washington. William Fitzhugh, George Plater III's father-in-law, recommended Boulton to the general, saying, "he is a masterly hand and I believe will execute your work in an elegant manner at least equal to any in America." The recommendation was probably based on Boulton's work at Sotterley. In May 1785, Washington contracted with Boulton to "finish the large room at the North end of the said dwelling house [Mount Vernon] in a plain and elegant manner; either of stucco, wainscot, or partly of both as the said George Washington shall direct." Washington then sent a ship to pick up Boulton's tools from Sotterley. As it happened, Boulton wrote Washington shortly thereafter, claiming that he could not fulfill the contract because of obligations to his creditors. Washington angrily wrote telling Boulton to honor the contract or "abide the consequences."

Washington suspected Boulton's real reasons. Fitzhugh had warned him that Boulton had a habit of associating with people who led him into idleness and excessive drinking. Washington had thought bringing Boulton to Virginia would remove him from those influences, but when Boulton returned from Mount Vernon, he told George Plater that he did not intend to fulfill the contract. In Plater's view, Boulton had no intention of leaving his "idle and drunken associates." It is said that about this time too, Boulton's wife passed away. In the end, Washington decided to drop the matter and wrote to Fitzhugh that he chose not to engage Boulton lest his bad example influence his other workmen.

Little is known of Boulton's later life. Perhaps he never overcame his drinking problem, though there is one other major work that Boulton may have completed: the entry hall and drawing room at Bushwood Manor in St. Mary's County. The shell alcoves and staircase banister at Bushwood, which burned down in 1933, were so similar to those at Sotterley that it seems probable the same person designed them. When these rooms at Bushwood were finished is uncertain. Boulton died in 1801 and is buried in an unmarked grave in Poplar Hill Episcopal Church in Valley Lee, Maryland.

8

An Eighteenth-Century Slave Community

ENSLAVED AFRICAN AMERICANS lived at Sotterley throughout the eighteenth century, but the few surviving estate inventories and tax records tell us little about them. The inventory of James Bowles's estate at his death in 1727 lists forty-one slaves—twenty-seven males (or with male names), and fourteen women. The imbalance between the sexes was typical of the early eighteenth century, when thousands of slaves were imported to the Chesapeake, most of them men capable of performing hard labor. Eight of the slaves were listed as being young. The relatively small value placed on them indicated that they were not yet of working age. Also listed as having little monetary value were three older slaves, probably beyond working age.

One who was listed as a "man servant" and given a relatively small value may have been old, or he might have been a white indentured servant whose limited time of service made him less valuable. We do not know how many whites beyond the five members of the Bowles family were living at Sotterley. It is very likely that several other whites were on hand to help oversee the slave population, but it is certain that the great majority of those living and working at Sotterley were African slaves.

Slaves were listed only by first name, which was also typical. Most of the names are English, and five had names that were evidently given them by Europeans, such as Congo and Pompy. Perhaps they had been imported directly from Africa, for documents show that James Bowles ordered slaves from the Royal African Company. Although records of the slave ships' arrival in Maryland have not been found, those names may indicate that his order arrived and that he kept a few of the slaves to work at Sotterley and sold the rest.

Most of Bowles's slaves appear to have been field laborers. Some were listed as living at the "home plantation," while others lived in slave quarters at Hogg Neck and Half Pone. Among the slaves at Sotterley itself, Dick and Towerhill were listed as carpenters. They were two of the three most valuable slaves and the only ones whose specific skills were noted. Five women and one man, who presumably cooked and did household work, were listed as living in the "dwelling house." The inventory includes a few items in the various slave quarters or cabins, such as "negroe bedding" and various cooking pots, but any other items in the slave quarters were not regarded as having enough value to warrant a listing.

No such detailed information survives concerning the slaves owned by George Plater II and George Plater III. According to the first federal census in 1790, George Plater IV had ninety-three slaves at Sotterley. Beyond the total number, the census does not provide other information. Since most—over 80 percent—of slave holdings in the Chesapeake numbered fewer than twenty, Sotterley contained one of the larger slave communities in southern Maryland at the end of the eighteenth century.

There is some indication that some of the men and women at Sotterley found slavery intolerable and tried to escape their bondage. Late in the Revolutionary War, when British troops raided Sotterley, several slaves either escaped or were taken away by the raiders. After the war, George Plater twice placed advertisements in the newspaper offering rewards for slaves who had run away. One of those notices involved a twenty-five-year-old slave named Towerhill, who escaped in late 1785 or early 1786. Might he have been a descendant of James Bowles's carpenter? Towerhill is such an unusual name that it is hard to consider it mere coincidence and suggests that several generations of an enslaved family worked at Sotterley during the tenures of Bowles and the Platers.

More detailed information about the slaves living at Sotterley at the end of the eighteenth century is available from the 1793 tax list for George Plater IV and from the inventory of his estate when he died in 1802. George IV's estate listed thirty-eight slaves by first name, age, and value—twenty men and eighteen women. By that time the slave trade had declined, and the slave population in the Chesapeake was almost exclusively native-born. The ratio of men to women at Sotterley was therefore typical of a more stable African American population in the Chesapeake.

The 1793 tax list provides the ages of seventy-eight slaves at Sotterley, fifteen fewer than the census taken in 1790. Twenty-two were younger than eight years, and fourteen were children between eight and fourteen. Fourteen were men between fifteen and forty-five, twelve were women between fifteen and thirty, and seventeen comprised a group of men over forty-five and women over thirty. Except for the fifteen missing from 1790, who may have been sold or moved to another plantation, the age distribution strengthens the theory that this was a relatively stable community, probably including several couples each with several children. Ten years later George IV's estate inventory again lists fewer slaves but with a similar age spread. The inventory continues the practice of giving only first names, but the recurrence of similar names in different generations implies that parents named their children after older generations. In addition, one notice for an escaped slave noted that "Clem" often referred to himself as "Clem Hill," suggesting that although white society referred to slaves only by their first names, some slaves adopted family names.

Neither George IV's inventory nor the 1793 tax list identified the skills of individual slaves, though George IV's will did specifically mention six slaves who were given to his wife. One of these, Sall, was said to be a cook. The others probably were household slaves.

Although we know little about the large slave community living at Sotterley for most of the eighteenth century, one thing is certain. Without their labor, George Plater and Sotterley would not have prospered. The crops would not have been raised nor the tobacco cured and packed. Richard Boulton may have performed the fine carpentry for the staircase and shell alcoves, but the trees would not have been felled or the house built without slave labor. The fine pine paneling in the house was undoubtedly cut and sawn by slaves. Perhaps someday research will shed more light on their lives, and their vital contributions.

Governor George Plater III.

9

George Plater:
Maryland Statesman

THE WAR transformed Maryland politics. In August 1776, when the special convention called to create a new state government met, George Plater was elected to the committee charged with drafting a Declaration of Rights and a Constitution. Overall, it was a convention inclined toward keeping the status quo. Plater himself was a member of a faction that represented the interests of the traditional landed gentry, who feared that in the unsettled political situation, unruly democratic elements would seize the opportunity to undermine economic and social stability.

The committee produced a generally conservative document but one that also included some surprisingly moderate provisions. It limited the suffrage to owners of property, placed still higher property qualifications on those seeking to hold office, and created a strong, indirectly elected Senate to check the actions of a more representative House of Delegates. Yet though they desired a conservative political system, the committee wrote strong civil rights protections into the state's Declaration of Rights and proposed two remarkably liberal provisions. One was that "all freemen" who met the property qualifications should have the franchise. That meant that the few free black men in Maryland who met the property qualifications were legally qualified to vote. The provision eventually was amended in 1802, after Plater's death, and blacks were banned from voting. A second proposed provision banned the importation of slaves into Maryland, but the convention chose not to retain this provision in the final constitution.

Although Plater supported both provisions, he was not among those who spoke of ending slavery altogether. His tobacco business, prosperity, and social status were based on slaves, who were considered property. When they escaped from Sotterley, he offered rewards for their capture and return, and he protested against the British and others who stole his slaves. In arguing for a pardon for a slave convicted of murder who was owned by a close friend he added: "I am not fond of having rogues escape punishment, but on the contrary should rather choose they should suffer as examples to others, particularly negroes, among whom villainy and roguery is but too common."

Once the members of the convention adopted the new state constitution, elections were held to select the officers for the new government. In November 1776, Plater won a five-year term as senator. His constituents re-elected him in 1781 and again in 1786. Soon after his return from the Continental Congress in December 1780, Plater gained the presidency of the Senate. Except for a few periods when he was granted leaves of absence, he continued as president of the Senate until his election as governor.

The Articles of Confederation, a purposely weak form of federal government, favored states' rights over any form of central authority. Among other things, it allowed each state to manage its own internal and external trade and economic affairs, a policy that quickly led to a growing dissatisfaction with the effects of competing state trade policies. Businessmen such as Plater understood the problem and advocated a stronger federal government. In 1786, Congress requested the states to send delegates to a convention in Philadelphia to consider the defects in the federal system created under the Articles. While the convention met in 1787, a debate raged in Maryland and elsewhere between those who supported a stronger federal government, the Federalists, and their opponents, the Anti-federalists. Although Plater clearly supported the Federalists he did not seek a seat at the Philadelphia convention.

Once the delegates adopted the new Constitution it had to be ratified by at least nine of the states. In November 1787 the Maryland Senate, with Plater presiding, voted to call a separate ratifying convention the following March. The House of Delegates voted to hold the convention in April, to allow more time for a "free and fair" consideration of the document. The House prevailed.

Plater penned a letter urging support for ratification. "If this plan is not adopted, we shall be in a much worse situation," he argued. "We shall be an object of ridicule at home & of contempt abroad—Our present government is found, by sad Experience, to want Energy & Efficiency; & though the proposed . . . may not please eviry Man . . . yet I believe it must be considered, to be the wisest & best under all circumstances. . . . Were I a member of the convention . . . I should not hesitate . . . to adopt it – trusting, as there is a proper door open, that the Congress may in the future make such amendments as to render it unexceptionally good." Plater ran as a candidate and was elected to Maryland's ratification convention.

By spring, six states had ratified the Constitution. Maryland was to be the first of the southern states to consider it, and George Washington believed ratification by Maryland was crucial to influence Virginia and undercut talk of a separate confederation of southern states. The convention opened on April 21. Behind the leadership of Judge Alexander Contee Hanson the Federalists, who dominated the proceedings, unanimously elected Plater president. Its pro-ratification majority then adopted procedures to limit debate and move rapidly toward final approval. Although William Paca, one of Maryland's signers of the Declaration of Independence, attempted to offer several amendments, the majority decided to vote on ratification first. Sixty-three of the seventy-four delegates cast their votes in favor of the new government, including Plater. The group then allowed Paca to present his amendments, but the convention voted to adjourn before considering them.

In January 1789, Plater was elected, with the second highest number of votes, to become one of eight Maryland electors to the first Electoral College. The electors met in February and unanimously supported Washington for president. Maryland was only entitled to six electoral votes, and Plater chose to defer and allow others to sign the vote on behalf of the state.

In 1790, a political struggle erupted in Maryland between those who supported the Congress's decision to build a new capital on the Potomac and those who promoted Baltimore as an alternative. Plater and a majority in the Senate supported the Congress's decision and in December 1791 the General Assembly passed legislation transferring Maryland's portion of the land for the new capital. In January, Plater, then serving as governor, signed the bill transferring the land to the federal government.

In November 1791, George Plater's supporters again unanimously elected him to the governor's chair. He served a short term, however, and his most significant action was signing the land transfer legislation. Plater had had health problems for several years, and on February 10, 1792, he died in Annapolis. According to contemporary accounts, his body was returned to Sotterley and buried in the family graveyard north of the main house, but his grave has not been found.

Newspapers in several states carried notices of his death and short eighteenth-century-style obituaries appeared in Annapolis and Baltimore publications. The *Maryland Journal and Baltimore Advertiser* praised Plater for "his uniformly just and dignified conduct in various important trusts," adding that he was "tenderly affectionate as a husband—kind and conciliating as a parent—steady and endearing as a friend—mild and compassionate as a master." To that writer and others, Plater epitomized the ideal of an eighteenth-century gentleman.

Plater's obituary in the Maryland Gazette.
Maryland State Archives.

10

The New Capital

D URING THE TWO DECADES following George Plater III's death, years known as the Federal period in American history, St. Mary's County experienced a wave of emigration. With limited land and changing economic conditions, the county grew less desirable for many. Numbers of freemen took their families and sometimes their slaves to new land in Maryland counties to the north and west, and to Kentucky. In the first federal census in 1790, the population of St. Mary's County's was 15,544. By 1810 it had fallen below 13,000, and it remained in that range for more than a century. For generations the sons and daughters of large St. Mary's families had to consider whether to remain at home or pursue opportunities elsewhere.

Because the Platers were wealthy, they were under no pressure to go west. When George died in 1792, his will divided his extensive land holdings among his three sons: George Plater IV, John Rousby Plater, and Thomas Plater. George IV received Sotterley and the other adjacent lands in Resurrection Manor. John acquired the lands in St. Joseph's Manor around what is now called Town Creek in St. Mary's County and property in Prince Georges County. His was the smallest of the bequests. Thomas got substantial property in Montgomery County. Each of George Plater's daughters received $3,000, a considerable sum for the time. George III's slaves were divided among his children with almost all going to George IV and John. Two of George and Elizabeth's children remained in St. Mary's, but three others moved to

Montgomery County and became involved in the development of the new federal city of Washington.

George III's prominence smoothed the way for each of his sons to get a start in social and public life, but none of them matched his accomplishments. George IV was elected to the Lower House of the Maryland Assembly in 1790, but he was not re-elected after 1793. A year after his father's death, the 1793 tax assessment indicated that George IV's land and possessions in what was then called Lower Resurrection Hundred made him the third-wealthiest planter in St. Mary's. The richest was Richard Barnes, owner of Tudor Hall, who had been his father's colleague in the General Assembly. Second was William Somerville, owner of Mulberry Fields and the executor of his father's estate. During 1794–95, George IV served as a justice of the peace in St. Mary's County, but his principal work was as a planter managing Sotterley. He followed his father in serving as a vestryman of St. Andrew's Parish from his father's death until his own passing.

George married Cecilia Bond in 1795. Together they had a son, George V, in 1796. After Cecilia died following the birth of her second child, George married Elizabeth Somerville, the daughter of William Somerville. They soon became the parents of a daughter, Ann Elizabeth, born in 1798. Family stories describe George as a handsome and elegant gentleman who was more interested in enjoying the pleasures of a wealthy planter's life than in minding the business of the plantation. Although the rising price of tobacco made the 1790s a period of prosperity for tobacco planters, George accumulated significant debts. When he died relatively young in 1802, most of his personal property, including many of his sixty-three slaves, had to be sold to settle his debts.

George's brothers, John and Thomas, became lawyers and had brief public careers. John stayed in St. Mary's; Thomas owned Bradford's Rest in Montgomery County and practiced law in Georgetown. The two daughters found husbands who became even more successful. Rebecca married Uriah Forrest in 1789. Although Forrest came from a St. Mary's family that was less socially prominent than the Platers, he was a Revolutionary War hero, who had lost a leg serving under George Washington in the disastrous battle of Germantown. After the war, Forrest established a merchant shipping business in Georgetown, where he had a home, now known as the Forrest-Marbury House. Uriah and Rebecca also had a house on an estate north of Georgetown known as Rosedale, where they raised five children.

In 1791, President George Washington chose a ten-mile-square tract including Georgetown to be the site of the nation's new capital. On March 29, Uriah and Rebecca Forrest hosted a dinner at their home in Georgetown for Washington and local landowners who had met that day to make arrangements for purchasing the land on which the Capitol, the President's House, and other buildings of the new federal city were to be constructed. Forrest is credited with playing an important role in the land transactions for the new capital. However, he was one of a group of landowners who had a falling out with Washington and sued him for breach of contract on a land deal. Eventually the dispute was settled.

In 1793, Forrest was elected to Congress, and in 1796 to the Maryland Senate. Like all the Platers, Forrest was a Federalist who supported strong central government. When the federal government moved to the new capital in 1800, the Forrests hosted a dinner to welcome President John Adams to Washington.

In 1790, Ann, then just sixteen, married Philip Barton Key, the son of a prominent planter family from Cecil County. During the Revolution, he had been a Loyalist who joined General Howe's forces in Philadelphia and fought for the British. Before the war ended he went to London to study law at the Inns of Court. He returned to Maryland after the war and practiced law in Leonardtown. George Plater III, a man who wished to heal the divisions of war, had no objection to his young daughter marrying a socially prominent, English-educated and aspiring lawyer, even though he had been a Loyalist. Perhaps because of his past, Philip and Ann

Ann Plater Key.
Courtesy of Philip Barton Key.

chose to hold their wedding on July 4, the anniversary of the Declaration of Independence. The couple lived in Annapolis before moving to the new District of Columbia near Rebecca and Uriah Forrest.

Key served in the Maryland House of Delegates from 1794 until 1800. He too was an ardent Federalist, and in recognition of his support, Adams, on the last night of his presidency, appointed Key chief judge of the new federal Fourth Circuit Court. When Thomas Jefferson became president in 1801 and the Republicans assumed power, they rescinded the Judiciary Act, depriving Key and the other "midnight judges" of their appointments. In 1805, in a precedent-setting case that confirmed the independence of the Supreme Court, Key was among the lawyers who successfully defended Associate Justice Samuel Chase, one of Maryland's signers of the Declaration of Independence, when Republicans impeached him on charges of treason. The following year, Key ran for election to Congress from Maryland's Third Congressional District, replacing Thomas Plater. He won and served three terms.

Despite the fact that their husbands had fought on opposite sides during the Revolution, the two sisters' families, living on adjoining estates, remained very close for the rest of their lives. When Washington real estate collapsed in 1797, and Uriah Forrest saw his fortune plummet and was on the verge of losing the family home at Rosedale, his brother-in-law came to his aid by agreeing to buy from them 250 acres in a part of Washington now known as Cleveland Park. There, on a hilltop overlooking the new federal buildings, Key built a new house for Ann, called Woodley. When the couple moved into Woodley in 1801, Philip was already, like Uriah Forrest, a leading citizen of the new federal city, and he and Ann made Woodley a social mecca known for its "great elegance and hospitality."

After Uriah Forrest's death in 1805, Rebecca remained owner of Rosedale but was troubled with many debts. Key again came to her aid by taking a mortgage on the estate. Ten years later, before his death, he forgave the mortgage, ensuring that Rebecca would be secure there for the rest of her life. (She died in 1843.) When Key died in 1815, Thomas Plater served as executor of his estate, and Ann remained the mistress of Woodley until she sold it in 1832. She died on December 18, 1834. For many years, the two sisters lived as widows on adjacent country estates in the new District of Columbia, but what they knew or thought of the difficulties facing their brother George IV and their nephew, young George V, at Sotterley is not recorded.

II

The War of 1812 and the End of the Plater Era

THE PLATER ERA at Sotterley ended in 1822. The traditional story of how the family lost Sotterley has it that George V was a ne'er-do-well, addicted to drink and gambling, who relinquished the estate with a roll of the dice at a gambling table. The truth was more complicated. A number of shifting winds affected Sotterley and the men responsible for her.

George V was just six when his father died in 1802. He and Sotterley were put under the guardianship of his uncle John Plater. Five years later, John also became the guardian of George's half sister Ann Elizabeth. Through inheritance from her father and grandfather, Ann too had substantial land, slaves, and property, for which her uncle became responsible. It is not clear whether George and Ann lived with their uncle John at Sotterley or on his property on nearby St. Joseph's Manor. For a time, George V was reported to be a boarding student at Charlotte Hall Academy.

John Plater had been educated at St. John's College in Annapolis. A lawyer, he served as a judge of the Orphans Court in St. Mary's County. He continued to live in St. Mary's and was a vestryman at St. Andrew's church from the death of George IV until George V reached age twenty-one. He was a prominent member of the Federalist Party in Maryland, and a St. Mary's County delegate in the Maryland House of Delegates for six one-year terms between 1805 and 1819. In 1813 he served briefly as Speaker pro tem. of the House of Delegates. In the presidential elections of 1796 and 1808, he was chosen by election to be a presidential elector in Maryland.

But agricultural and trade patterns were changing in Maryland at the beginning of the nineteenth century. After the Revolution, Americans were not bound exclusively to established trade channels with Great Britain and had to adjust to a more complicated international market. Tobacco was no longer the only cash crop, for wheat had gradually become a profitable grain. Wheat required different investments and farming methods. Moreover, Baltimore merchants had taken over the marketing of both tobacco and wheat from plantations in St. Mary's County, and tobacco was no longer shipped directly from the wharf at Sotterley. The century during which Sotterley Creek had been a hub for the plantation's international trade was over. It appears that George IV, John Plater, and young George V were not adept at adjusting to changing times.

The Napoleonic Wars in Europe created challenges for Baltimore merchants and Chesapeake planters alike. Britain and France each sought to weaken the other by restricting and disrupting trade, and British ships frequently impressed American sailors on American ships, claiming they were deserters from the His Majesty's Navy. In response, President Jefferson adopted a trade embargo in 1807 that banned all exports from the United States. Unfortunately, the embargo did not keep the country out of what became known as the War of 1812. Federalists from Maryland, Philip Barton Key prominent among them, had opposed the embargo and the idea of war in part because of the impact on Maryland's trade, but they were outvoted, and it was not long before the war came to Maryland.

In 1813 and again in 1814, British forces sailed up Chesapeake Bay and raided plantations for supplies. Plantations that resisted were burned; those that did not had their grain and livestock purchased at command prices or seized outright. British warships anchored near Sotterley and reportedly obtained livestock along the south side of the Patuxent. In the summer of 1814, during the British campaign to attack Washington, John Plater reported that his crops were ruined by "depredations of the enemy." That year, about forty slaves owned by the Platers escaped to British ships in response to British offers of freedom.

In June 1814 a naval battle took place across the Patuxent from Sotterley that spilled onto Plater land. Commodore Joshua Barney's flotilla had taken refuge in St. Leonard's Creek, where British warships could not maneuver, and militiamen assembled at Sotterley to be ferried across the Patuxent to reinforce the troops supporting Barney. The British arrived on June 10, and on the thirteenth landed troops from one warship on the south bank of the Patuxent "to oppose three hundred militia collected near the house of Mr. Prater [Plater]." The next day the same force landed again somewhere on Plater's land and burned a tobacco barn and house that had been used by the militia.

Separately on June 14, a Captain Brown led about a hundred British soldiers from HMS *Loire* to the main house at Sotterley and reported finding that the livestock, slaves, and furnishings had been sent away. John Plater was the only person at the house. Brown reported that he offered to pay for Sotterley's poultry, but Plater refused payment. Brown then ordered his men to guard the entrances to the house while the poultry was seized and warned Plater that he need not be concerned in the future, because his property would not be harmed unless it was used by the militia. Since the British had burned other houses on the Patuxent for being hospitable to American militia, why they spared the main house at Sotterley is not clear, for they knew that some parts of Plater's land had been used by the militia earlier. Although the main house survived, the Platers nevertheless suffered substantial losses during the British campaign.

The Platers were not involved in the fighting in Maryland. There is no record that John Plater served as an officer in the militia as had his brother and father, though he once reported being away on militia duty. Nor is there any indication that George V, who was eighteen when the British landed and marched on Washington, joined the resistance. But some other members of the extended family were involved. John Plater was one of ten county leaders to petition the state in 1813 to send forces to help the militia defend St. Mary's County. In August, when the British captured Washington, Ann and Philip Barton Key would have been able to see the fires of the burning White House and Capitol from their Woodley estate overlooking the city. Most importantly for American history, the defense of Baltimore a month later inspired Philip Barton Key's nephew, Francis Scott Key, to write "The Star-Spangled Banner."

In 1802, at George IV's death, much of Sotterley's property had to be sold to settle his debts. The main house was said to be in "reasonably good repair," but many of the buildings in the other quarters of the property were "not habitable" or "not worth repairing." Under John Plater's stewardship, Sotterley's decline worsened. The annual guardianship reports state that property was sold to cover expenses, losses, and repairs of various kinds. Some of the sales were to John himself. The decline was also reflected in the number of slaves at Sotterley. At his death, George IV held sixty-three slaves. In 1820, three years after George V reached his maturity, but twenty remained. On the other hand, John and his son had accumulated a total of ninety-seven slaves. At age twenty-one, George IV was in debt to his guardian for over $3,000. It appears that a significant transfer of wealth from Sotterley to John Plater occurred during his guardianship. No one seems to have raised any questions about it.

Likewise, Ann's considerable inheritance declined under John Plater's guardianship. When Ann was about twenty, she married her first cousin John Rousby Plater Jr. Whether it was a marriage of love or convenience is not clear, but by law her remaining property became her husband's.

By the time he was twenty-one, George V appears not only to have gained control of Sotterley but initially to have benefited from his family's social position. He served as a vestryman at St. Andrew's Church from 1818 to 1822, and in 1820 he was elected to the House of Delegates. But just two years after he became responsible for Sotterley, the postwar economic boom turned into the nation's first recession, the terrible Panic of 1819, which depressed the price of tobacco for several years. Faced with debts and low prices for his major cash crop, George V chose to mortgage Sotterley to John Plater and sell various other tracts. To what extent his difficulties were the result of, or caused, by his penchants for alcohol and gambling is uncertain, but in 1822 he finally sold Sotterley and all the remaining lands of Resurrection Manor to William C. Somerville, the son of the executor of his grandfather's estate, for $29,000 and probably used the proceeds to settle his debts. Why he chose to sell to Somerville rather than to John Plater or another member of his family is unclear.

It appears that George V never recovered from the tragedy—and humiliation—of losing Sotterley. No records show how he lived the remainder of his days. In 1846 he died and was buried in a private graveyard at Bloomsbury, the estate south of Leonardtown belonging to his cousin Edward Plater, a son of John Rousby Plater Sr.

The end of the Plater era is a complex story and one that is only partially available from existing records. Nevertheless, it seems certain that although George V was not up to the challenge of sustaining Sotterley during this difficult period, John Plater bears much of the responsibility for its decline.

12

A Southern Farmer

Soon after buying George V's property, William C. Somerville sold a thousand acres, including Sotterley, to Thomas Barber. In 1826, Barber died, providing in his will that Sotterley should be divided "share and share alike" between his daughter Lydia and his stepdaughter Emeline Dallum. Emeline was given four hundred acres including Sotterley, and Lydia received six hundred adjoining acres on Fenwick Manor. Each share was valued at $7,000. Lydia married Chapman Billingsley, and the couple lived at Lydia's home.

A few weeks before Thomas Barber's death, Emeline had married Dr. Walter Hanson Stone Briscoe of Charles County, a graduate of Charlotte Hall School who had gone on to study medicine under Dr. N. R. Smith. Where Doctor Briscoe and Emeline first lived and just when they moved to Sotterley is unclear, but move they did to take advantage of the land and house Emeline had inherited. For sixty years, Briscoe managed the farm at Sotterley and practiced medicine in the community.

At the time Doctor Briscoe moved to Sotterley, St. Mary's County remained a rural society that maintained traditions from its seventeenth- and eighteenth-century origins. The economic and demographic trends that were changing Maryland and the nation had had little impact on the county's social and economic life, which continued to be led by a few landed, slave-owning families. Still, the shift from the Platers to the Briscoes shows that the identities of the leading families did change over time, and change appeared

Walter Hanson Stone Briscoe.

elsewhere in the county as well. Leonardtown was experiencing a degree of growth. It got its first local newspaper, the *St. Mary's Beacon,* in 1839, and by the 1850s its population numbered about five hundred. Although the editor still referred to Leonardtown as a "village," the founding of the paper and the coming of regular steamship service in the 1830s were steps toward the county seat becoming a town.

Walter and Emeline made substantial changes to the main house. In the nineteenth century, travel within St. Mary's County was principally by dirt road rather than by water. The Briscoes added the covered porches on the west or land side of the house and used a door on that side as their main entrance. A hitching post for horses still stands by that door. They also added a two-story addition on the east or river side of the house that contained a new kitchen adjoining the room they used as their dining room. The Briscoes also acquired many elegant pieces of eighteenth- and nineteenth-century furniture for their home.

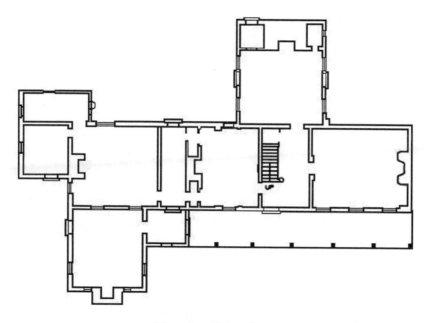

Floor plan of Briscoe house.

Tobacco continued to be the farm's principal cash crop before the Civil War, but it was no longer grown on rotating tobacco fields. The introduction of wheat had led to the clearing and plowing of fields, and tobacco, wheat, and clover were now often planted in rotation. Manure was used as fertilizer, and the clover crop was plowed under to enrich the soil. Corn was generally grown on separate fields. Records indicate that tobacco, wheat, and corn were grown at Sotterley along with other minor crops. Doctor Briscoe also raised some cotton, hogs, and sheep, for wool and slaughter. He acquired an additional three hundred acres called Hectors and later sold this to his son-in-law Thomas Bond. In turn he bought from Bond the 320-acre Half Pone farm.

Steamboats began offering regular service along the Patuxent about 1830, and a steamboat wharf was built on the point just south of Sotterley Creek. Hogsheads of tobacco were now taken by ox cart to the Sotterley Wharf to be shipped to Baltimore for inspection and sale. Gradually, Sotterley Wharf became a hub linking the area around the farm to Baltimore.

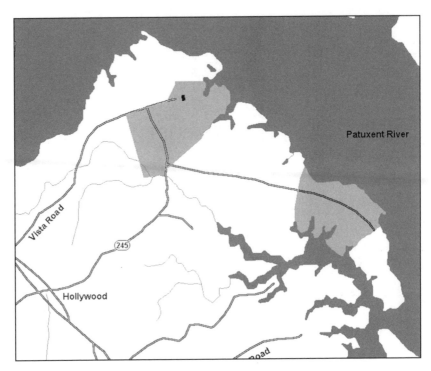

Walter Hanson Stone Briscoe's land in 1885.
Courtesy, Peter Himmelheber.

Slave labor still cultivated tobacco. According to the 1850 census, 6,223 whites, 5,842 slaves, and 1,623 free blacks lived in St. Mary's County. At the time of his marriage, Doctor Briscoe owned about ten slaves. He bought more, for in the 1850 census he was recorded as owning thirty-four. Unfortunately, the few of his letters that have been found do not shed light on his views about slavery, whether he saw it as a "necessary evil" as many in the South did, or how he reconciled slaveholding with his deeply held religious beliefs.

Although with seven hundred acres and thirty slaves remaining Sotterley had shrunk from the time Governor Plater owned it, the Briscoes were among the wealthiest families of antebellum St. Mary's County. They were part of the local elite and could trace their roots in southern Maryland back to the colony's founding. In the 1830s, Briscoe served on the levy court, which functioned as the county administration before the county commissioner system was introduced in 1839.

Like the Platers, the Briscoes were Episcopalians and members of St. Andrew's Church. Doctor Briscoe served as a vestryman there from 1829 until his death. When St. Andrew's decided to hold a second auction of the church's pews, Briscoe's purchase of pews numbers one and two served to demonstrate his importance in the parish hierarchy. His obituary described him as a strict Episcopalian who appeared "to be ever walking in his 'great taskmaster's eye.'" After his death the vestry paid tribute to him, noting that his "life was marked by a Christian spirit and conscientious service." Walter, Emeline, and other members of the family are buried in the family plot prominently located in front of the church.

In the years before the Civil War, blessed with a happy marriage, the Briscoes created a warm home atmosphere bustling with children. In 1850, after their twelfth child had been born, Doctor Briscoe wrote a friend that "the old woman looks like she might bear another and another blessing yet, though . . . I dare say she would be content for those blessings to stop but it is not for us to prescribe the limits." In that era, family planning was not yet understood. A little over a year later, Emeline gave birth to her last child, Walter Hanson Stone Briscoe Jr.

The Briscoes were dedicated to all their children's education. Several of the boys were sent to Charlotte Hall School. Henry reportedly attended the Maryland medical college in Baltimore to obtain his medical training; David studied law at the University of Virginia. To ensure that their five daughters were also educated, the Briscoes established a school at Sotterley during the 1840s and 1850s. It was in a one-room schoolhouse located near the front yard. The Briscoes invited their friends from neighboring counties to board their daughters at Sotterley so they could attend the school, and turned the bedroom over the drawing room into a dormitory. Although the school was for girls, some of the Briscoes' sons also attended. Mary Blades, the Briscoes' governess, taught the school in the late 1840s. Mrs. Kate Thomas, who attended it, recalls that the girls had quite a lot of fun amusing themselves with music and dancing, pastimes the doctor found foolish.

In the 1850s, St. Mary's County was a stable but not growing agricultural society still heavily dependent on the institution of slavery. Sotterley enjoyed relative prosperity, and the Briscoes enjoyed a tranquil and happy life. But beyond their horizon, the issues of slavery and abolition were disturbing the nation and sowing seeds discord.

Mary Blades

Born in 1814 in Caroline County, Mary Blades came to Sotterley in the 1840s, initially as the tutor for the Briscoe children. When the Briscoes established a school at Sotterley, Mary became its teacher and stayed at least through 1850. She taught grammar, reading, and arithmetic and gained a reputation as a "martinet" in the classroom.

When the St. Mary's Female Seminary, the predecessor of St. Mary's College, opened in 1847, Mary was offered a position as teacher but turned it down, preferring to remain at Sotterley. In 1852 she agreed to become principal at the seminary only to resign a year later, after which the seminary closed for a few years. In 1858, Miss Blades returned to the position of co-principal of the seminary, serving under the newly elected president of the board, the Briscoes' neighbor, Colonel Chapman Billingsley.

Mary reportedly "possessed remarkable charm for the opposite sex." After rejecting numerous suitors and waiting into her forties, in 1860 she married Colonel Richard Miles of St. Mary's County, a devout Catholic. Mary converted to Catholicism, and left the seminary that year.

In 1884, Colonel and Mrs. Miles donated Rose Hill Farm to the Catholic Church as the site for a girls' school. Rose Hill Farm was located in the southeast quadrant of the intersection of routes 5 and 245, which is now the Leonardtown campus of the College of Southern Maryland. In 1885, St. Mary's Academy was opened on that site. Mary Blades died on January 17, 1886, and is buried at Sacred Heart Catholic Church in Bushwood.

Mary Blades Miles. From, Loretta Norris and Anne Tennison, "St. Mary's Academy," in Chronicles of St. Mary's, *51 (Summer 2003).*

13

The Civil War

Slavery, an institution that had been basic to the Chesapeake economy for more than 150 years, had by the 1850s created an irreconcilable conflict in the nation. In 1857, Chief Justice Roger B. Taney, a Marylander, wrote the infamous Dred Scott decision, declaring that blacks were not eligible for citizenship. Coming as it did on the heels of bloody fighting over slavery in the Kansas Territory, the case enraged many in the North. When two years later John Brown, who had gained a violent reputation in Kansas, made an unsuccessful attempt to seize the U.S. Arsenal at Harper's Ferry, Virginia, and instigate a slave rebellion, the South was terrified and alarmed. What Walter Briscoe thought of these events is unknown, but as one of the larger slave owners in the county, he is said to have opposed abolition.

In the spring of 1860, the Democratic Party split over slavery. In the presidential election that fall, John Breckinridge, the candidate of the party's Southern wing, swept St. Mary's County and won the state of Maryland but lost the election to Republican Abraham Lincoln. Few in the South had voted for the "Black Republican" candidate, and in St. Mary's County, Lincoln received just one vote. Yet even with a secret ballot, there can be little doubt how Doctor Briscoe had voted.

In December, a month after Lincoln's election, South Carolina seceded from the Union. Other states followed. On February 8, 1861, seven states in the deep South formed the Confederate States of America.

A few days later, the *St. Mary's Beacon* reported the formation of "Smallwood's Vigilantes" and listed Doctor Briscoe as its surgeon. Nothing more is known of this group, which appears to have been one of many local outfits forming in the South to resist Lincoln's policies. Whether Briscoe agreed to his appointment is not known.

On April 12, Confederate batteries in Charleston opened fire on Fort Sumter. President Lincoln responded by calling the nation to arms to quell the insurrection, prompting Virginia to secede and join the Confederacy on April 17. At this juncture, Maryland became geographically crucial to the federal government, because its secession would leave Washington surrounded by Confederate states. On April 19, a riot occurred in Baltimore when a mob attempted to block a regiment of Massachusetts volunteers from passing through the city to Washington. Secessionist sentiment peaked in the city, and as news of events there spread, inflamed many parts of the state.

In this charged atmosphere, what was said to be the largest public meeting ever held in St. Mary's County saw eight hundred citizens assemble in Leonardtown on April 23 for the purpose of "considering the present crisis and adopting measures for the defense of our rights, the security of our homes and the maintenance of the honor of our state." Chapman Billingsley, Briscoe's neighbor, was one of the organizers. Secessionist sentiment was in full fury that day. The meeting resolved that the county commissioners should be asked to provide $10,000 to purchase arms with which the citizens could defend themselves. The meeting sent a committee of three, including Walter Briscoe, to secure the commissioners' agreement, which they did. Although Doctor Briscoe was not appointed to the committee formed to implement the meeting's resolutions, it is likely that he agreed with many of its resolves. In the ensuing weeks, secessionist sentiment subsided, the legislature took no action, and Maryland remained in the Union.

Three of Dr. Briscoe's sons crossed the Potomac to fight for the Confederacy. Dr. Henry Briscoe was commissioned in the Confederate army in 1862 and assigned as a surgeon in Richmond. In 1863 he was transferred to Wilmington, North Carolina, to organize a military hospital there, then assigned in 1864 to the 26th Virginia Regiment where he remained for the duration of the war. Chapman Briscoe served as a sergeant in the 1st Maryland Infantry. In March 1864, David Briscoe was commissioned as a third lieutenant in Company D, 43rd Battalion, Virginia Cavalry. Due to casualties in the unit, David became the company commander by the end of the war. Although

Lieutenant Briscoe was seriously wounded near Petersburg, all three brothers survived the war and returned to Maryland. Another son, either Samuel or James, was also in the South for at least part of the war, but there is no record that either served in the Confederate forces.

At age sixty, Doctor Briscoe remained at home. He and Emeline were undoubtedly concerned for their sons' safety, about the presence of Union troops in the county, and over the impact of the war on their slaves. There is no indication that he actively engaged in espionage for the Confederacy, but the family was under suspicion like many others in St. Mary's because it had sons fighting for the South. On Christmas day 1863, John Briscoe, then sixteen, was arrested in Leonardtown and charged with attempting to purchase goods for the enemy and lying about it. John told the authorities that he had done nothing more than place an order for gloves for his brother David, who was then in the South. Whatever his real purpose, John was released, but the warning was clear.

Union troops occasionally visited Sotterley. A century after the war, Mabel Ingalls, the last owner of Sotterley, recalled hearing Mrs. Sarah Briscoe Thomas, Doctor Briscoe's daughter, tell her parents Herbert and Louisa Satterlee about a hiding place in the paneling in "Madame Bowles's Chamber," where documents and valuables were hidden during the war. Sarah was a young woman living at home during the war and was recounting this story fifty years after it had ended when young Mabel overheard her. She in turn recorded it fifty years later, so although it is a family story and plausible, it has not been confirmed by other contemporary sources. That said, Herbert Satterlee, who bought Sotterley in 1910, found a removable panel covering a hiding place in that room. The Union officers who came to St. Mary's considered its slave owners to be "unscrupulous" and "secessionists." Sarah Thomas also said that when Union troops visited the family hid Doctor Briscoe in the attic over the kitchen out of the fear that he would be rude to them and provoke retribution on Sotterley.

In 1863, Lincoln authorized the enlistment of black soldiers to support the Union. The law limited recruitment to free blacks and slaves whose masters gave them permission to join. In practice, recruiters enticed slaves to run away and join the regiments of U.S. Colored Troops then organizing. In September 1863, Colonel William Birney was given the responsibility of recruiting black troops in Maryland. A month later, John Sothoron, the owner of the Plains plantation on the Patuxent north of Sotterley, shot one of Birney's lieutenants for encouraging slave desertions.

Infantry company, U.S. Colored Troops. Library of Congress.

No such violence occurred at Sotterley, but one of Briscoe's slaves, whose name was George Briscoe, did run away to enlist and in October 1863 became a member of Company J, 7th Regiment U.S.C.T.. It is the only documented instance of a slave leaving Sotterley during the war. The 7th Regiment was sent to Florida where it was commended as the best regiment in the service and an "example of unflagging energy and steady purpose." In August 1864, the regiment was committed to the last great battle of the Civil War, fought around Petersburg south of Richmond.

It happened that at the same time, Dr. Henry Briscoe was serving with the 26th Virginia in the Confederate lines before Petersburg. Both men are recorded as having been "in the trenches" for several months during the epic

Union siege of the city, which began in the summer of 1864 and lasted until the spring of 1865. How close the two came to meeting is unknown, but they met entirely different fates. Dr. Henry Briscoe was the more fortunate. After abandoning Petersburg, his unit retreated to Appomattox Court House, where Robert E. Lee surrendered the Army of Northern Virginia. Henry was paroled and permitted to return to Maryland. After Appomattox, George Briscoe's regiment was sent to garrison duty in Texas, and Company J was stationed as a police force in Indianola. There George Biscoe died on October 18, 1866, of cholera.

The war doomed slavery in Maryland. In 1862, Congress ended slavery in the District of Columbia, an action that prompted many slaves to escape from surrounding Maryland. Lincoln's Emancipation Proclamation in 1863 freed the slaves only in territory under Confederate control, but in 1864 a state convention dominated by Unionists rewrote Maryland's constitution and added Article 24 to the Declaration of Rights. It banned slavery and freed all slaves in Maryland. In the vote on the constitutional amendments, St. Mary's countians voted 1,078 to 99 against ratification. Again, it is likely that Doctor Briscoe voted with the majority. Nevertheless, the amendments were ratified, in large part because, in the first-ever use of absentee balloting in Maryland, soldiers serving with the Union armies were permitted to vote, and they voted overwhelmingly for emancipation.

Although the state did not authorize compensation for the owners of freed slaves, the possibility of federal compensation was still under discussion. Consequently, Dr. Briscoe compiled a detailed list of the fifty-three slaves he had owned at the time of emancipation. The 1850 federal census had recorded thirty-four slaves at Sotterley, and the 1860 census thirty-one. What was behind the large discrepancy between 1860 and 1864 is not clear.

The Civil War and emancipation freed the slaves at Sotterley and changed the economics of tobacco. How much the economy and society of St. Mary's would change remained to be seen.

Agnes Kane Callum.

14

The Kane Family

O UR KNOWLEDGE of the enslaved men, women, and families who lived and worked at Sotterley in the forty years before the Civil War is limited. We do know that Hillery Kane and his family were slaves then and that they remained at Sotterley for several years after emancipation before leaving to make new lives elsewhere in the county. We know of this family thanks to path-breaking research and family oral histories collected by Hillery's great-granddaughter, historian Agnes Kane Callum of Baltimore.

Hillery Kane was born in 1818 to Raphael Kane and Clara, who were slaves owned by different masters. Hillery lived with his mother on the plantation owned by William Neale of Jeremiah and was about eight when his mother was sold to another plantation. A year later in 1827, Hillery was given to James J. Gough to settle a debt. On Gough's plantation, he learned the craft of plastering. In 1837 he married another of Gough's slaves, fourteen-year-old Mariah. Records indicate that they probably had six children. The youngest, Frank, was born in 1848, the year in which Gough died. When Gough's estate was liquidated, Hillery Kane, his wife and three remaining children were put on the auction block in Leonardtown. Chapman Billingsley bought Hillery in 1848 for six hundred dollars, a price that reflected his age, health, and skills. No one present offered an acceptable price for Mariah, but the following year, Doctor Briscoe bought her and her children. By arrangement between

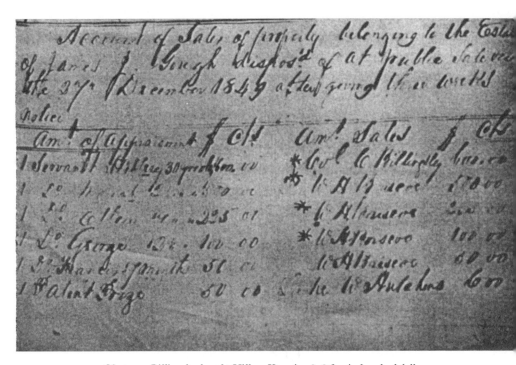

Chapman Billingsley bought Hillery Kane in 1848 for six hundred dollars.
Maryland State Archives.

Briscoe and Colonel Billingsley, Hillery was permitted to reside at Sotterley with his family.

A few years later, after Mariah passed away, Hillery married Alice Elsa Bond, then age fifteen. It is unclear whether Doctor Briscoe bought Elsa to allow Hillery to live with his new wife or whether she had been living at Sotterley before they decided to marry. They are believed to have had twelve children, all born in a small cabin at Sotterley. Elsa became a spinner and laundress, cleaning and ironing clothes for the Briscoes and for the girls attending their school. As was typical, Elsa passed these skills on to her daughters.

With more than thirty slaves living at Sotterley and nearly as many on Colonel Billingsley's adjoining property, the two farms were home to one of the larger slave communities in the county. At the time, it was not unusual in St. Mary's for slave families to be kept together.

Hillery was often away from Sotterley, because Colonel Billingsley rented him out for plastering jobs. As the mixed crop agriculture in antebellum southern Maryland did not keep slaves employed year-round, it was a common practice for owners to hire them out for the income they would bring. It has been said that Hillery Kane plastered many of the finest homes in St. Mary's County.

The Kane family lived in a slave cabin near the "big house." Some accounts indicate that there were several cabins along the rolling road, but no evidence of a row of cabins in this area has been found. Accounts from 1910 speak of seven or eight former slave cabins in different locations around the plantation. The sole remaining slave cabin on the rolling road was constructed in a manner common in the 1830s. Its walls were hewn and sawn logs with clay and mortar filling the spaces between the timbers. The one-room cabin had two doors but no windows on the first floor, and a loft with shuttered window openings. The floor was hard-packed dirt. The sixteen-by-eighteen-foot cabin was relatively large for such buildings and well constructed for the times, a testament to the slaves who built it. Its brick chimney was unusual for a slave dwelling.

Sotterley's slave cabin.

There is a story of hog killing time on the plantation, when slaves collected the bristles that were scraped from the skin of the newly slaughtered hog. When mixed with clay and salt from the river, these bristles served as important "chinking" between the cabin's rough-hewn logs for the winter months. When Hillery was with his family at Sotterley and not laboring in the fields, he made furniture and musical instruments. It has been said that Hillery made several beds, chairs, and tables for the cabin.

According to family lore, Hillery was also knowledgeable about the medicinal use of herbs and roots in the treatment of a variety of ailments, and was considered the slaves' "doctor." For food the family cooked the rations of fatty pork and corn that were regularly issued at the back door of the main house on Saturdays, and hunted for rabbit, deer, and possum to supplement those rations. On Sundays the Kanes, though Catholic, attended St. Andrew's Episcopal Church along with the Briscoes and Billingsleys. Although slaves were required to stand at the back, going to church was a welcome opportunity to socialize with slaves from other farms.

Frank Kane, Hillery's son, bought in 1849 for fifty dollars, served as Doctor Briscoe's carriage boy. The work involved driving the doctor on his business about the county and caring for his carriage horse, from which experience he learned animal husbandry. Frank's daughter, Julia Kane Jordan, recalled that her father liked to talk about his life at Sotterley and of his relationship with Doctor Briscoe. When Frank was about twelve, he and his family received orders to dress presentably and come to the front of the "big house." He and his brothers and sisters stood in line as Doctor Briscoe walked around them several times, inspecting them. The doctor said nothing and finally dismissed them. Back in their cabin, the family speculated about being sold. In the years before the Civil War, many slaves from the Chesapeake region were sold to work in southern cotton fields, but the Kanes did not suffer that fate. Later that week while driving the doctor's carriage, Frank reportedly told the doctor that he "dared not inquire . . . if he intended to sell the Kanes, but . . . if he had a master whom he served faithfully and the master had plans to sell him, then he would never serve that master again." Briscoe must have been surprised to hear such bluntness from someone so young, for he reportedly listened but did not reply.

As a carriage boy, Frank had the opportunity to see many places in the county. According to one story, despite his young age, Frank was sent alone to Baltimore one day to pick up bibles for Doctor Briscoe. It was a task that involved considerable responsibility and would have involved a few days' travel to Baltimore, an overnight stay in the city, and another long return trip by wagon. At the time, Baltimore had the largest population of free blacks in the country, about 35,000. If one wonders why Frank did not seize the opportunity to escape, his daughter remembers him saying that he did not want to leave his family, an understandable attitude for a very young boy. After emancipation, Frank earned his living by animal husbandry.

On November 1, 1864, by virtue of Maryland's new constitution, all the slaves at Sotterley became free. In thinking about her ancestors' experience under slavery, Agnes Kane Callum has said they should be remembered for having the strength and wisdom to survive an inherently cruel system, one in which families were often separated and some were occasionally lynched. Their strength of character has passed down to her generation. She also said that she has come across no evidence of beatings, whippings, or cruelty to slaves at Sotterley.

Although emancipation gave slaves their freedom, it did not alter many aspects of life in southern Maryland. The social and economic gap between the races changed only slowly. Many whites in southern Maryland maintained their paternalistic and racist attitudes towards blacks. After the war, Maryland took the first serious steps to develop elementary public education throughout the state, but equal public education for blacks would not be available until a century later.

It appears that many former slaves remained at Sotterley for a time after emancipation, working for some combination of room, board, and wages. The Kane family stayed. After the war, when Frank informed Doctor Briscoe of his plan to marry, the doctor offered to host the wedding in the mansion. On February 22, 1868, Frank Kane married Evelina Stewart. The bride, also a former slave, had been owned by Chapman Billingsley. Rev. Reginald. H. Murphy, the pastor at St. Andrew's Episcopal Church, performed the service, which meant that the marriage was consecrated by the church and recognized by the state, in contrast to slave weddings of the past that were only unofficially blessed by itinerant preachers. The wedding was one instance of social change at Sotterley, but since it is the only such wedding known to have taken place there, it probably was a reflection of Doctor Briscoe's special fondness for Frank Kane. Sweet water and sweet bread were served in the parlor to black and white guests, and afterwards the Kanes continued with dancing at their cabin. By 1874, Frank and Evelina had four children born at Sotterley. Evelina died in 1876 and may have been buried in a former slave graveyard located "not far from the slave quarter and near a stream."

Although Hillery Kane had been a Catholic when owned by the Catholic Gough family, he attended St. Andrew's Church while owned by the Briscoes. Sometime after emancipation, Hillery and many of his children began attending St. Nicholas Catholic Church in Jarboesville, now Lexington Park.

The youngest of Hillery's children, Sam Kane, was born at Sotterley in 1874. Around 1879, Hillery and Elsa left Sotterley for a new home nearby in Hollywood. Kane descendants believe that Hillery had remained at Sotterley partly out of loyalty to Doctor Briscoe and partly because it took years to save the money needed to buy a home. Frank Kane married his second wife, Caroline Thomas, in 1880; their children were not born at Sotterley. Hillery died around 1889, four years after Doctor Briscoe's death.

15

Rescued from Ruin

HOW MUCH the Briscoes' life changed after the Civil War is not clear. It appears that Doctor Briscoe accepted emancipation with equanimity and continued to devote himself to agriculture, though he raised less tobacco. Corn and wheat became the main cash crops, and with fertile soil and many former slaves staying on as tenants, Sotterley managed to sustain itself. In 1875, Doctor Briscoe became the Patuxent District representative of the Grange, a nationwide organization formed to improve the economic and social position of farm families. In time, most of the Briscoe children left. Henry continued his medical practice in Chaptico. David moved to Baltimore and established a law practice. James became an Episcopal pastor and began his service in Baltimore. The daughters married and moved away.

Among the children, Jeanette made the greatest contribution to the local community. In 1854 she had married Richard Thomas and moved to the Thomas estate at Deep Falls in St. Mary's County, but her love was education. The years following the war saw education develop in Maryland. In 1865, St. Mary's County instituted its first functioning public education program, but only for those who were white and, primarily, boys. The St. Mary's Female Seminary, which had struggled before the war, reopened in a more promising atmosphere. In 1868 the state provided scholarships for one student from each Maryland county to attend the seminary. Jeanette was elected to become its principal in 1872, and she awarded the institution's first graduation certificate in 1874. Jeanette served until her untimely death in 1881, but her daughter, Anne Elizabeth Thomas Lilburn, succeeded her until 1895. It was during the nearly quarter-century of this mother and daughter's leadership that the seminary established itself as a successful nondenominational school. It was also in this period, that Mary Blades Miles donated the land on which the new St. Mary's Academy, a Catholic school for girls, opened in 1885. Both Jeanette and Mary traced their educational accomplishments back to Doctor Briscoe's one-room school at Sotterley.

In the first decades after the war, the Democratic Party revived and dominated politics in Maryland. In St. Mary's County, it stood for preserving the traditional, that is, antebellum, economic and social system. Doctor Briscoe did not hold any public or party office after the war, but his obituary in the *St. Mary's Beacon*, a Democratic paper, praised him for being a lifelong party member. Benjamin Qwinn Harris, a prominent Democrat who had served in Congress during the war and become a symbol of wartime resistance to the federal government in southern Maryland, was the lead pallbearer at his funeral.

When Doctor Briscoe died in 1885, he left all his property to "beloved" Emeline, "my true, faithful and affectionate wife" for the rest of her life. After her death, the farm at Half Pone and much of the furniture at Sotterley was given to their youngest son, Walter Jr., "in appreciation of, and award for, his long and laborious efforts on our behalf." Walter was the only son who had taken to farming, and he remained with them at Sotterley. The rest of the estate was to be divided equally among his other children.

The obituary published in the *Beacon*, praised his character as follows: "Though ever walking quietly and unostentatiously, Doctor Briscoe arrested attention by his promptness and regularity in discharging neighborhood, religious and public obligations. He was a man of strictest methods in his habits and dealings, demanding no more than was right but exacting what was due him. He was somewhat stern and brusque of manner, but those who knew him best, and especially his neighbors, represent this as a mere crust which covered great kindness of heart and a hand liberal in secret charities."

After his father's death, Walter managed Sotterley until 1893. Emeline died in 1887, and their son, Rev. James Briscoe, bought Sotterley from the estate. Since Reverend Briscoe lived in Baltimore, Walter managed Sotterley for his brother until in 1893 he moved permanently to Half Pone. Walter's only son, John H. T. Briscoe, born in 1890, was the last child born in the main house at Sotterley. After Reverend Briscoe's death in 1904, his children, Elizabeth Briscoe Cashner and James Briscoe, inherited Sotterley. Elizabeth and her husband, J. D. Cashner, bought out James' share.

The last decades of the nineteenth century did not offer prosperous times in St. Mary's County. The industrial revolution that was transforming the United States into the world's leading manufacturing nation had little impact there. The period known as the Gilded Age for the great fortunes made elsewhere left southern Maryland agricultural and relatively poor. St. Mary's, which had contained about 6 percent of Maryland's population in the first federal census, had less than 1.5 percent in 1900.

One-year-old John H. T. Briscoe at Sotterley.

During Sotterley's Cashner years, seven or eight former slave cabins remained on land owned earlier by the Briscoes and Billingsleys. Several were still being used as homes by black families, including those of James Scriber, Ned Lyles, Alfred Edwards, Walter Barber, and others. In 1910, "Aunt" Nannie Williams was living in the slave cabin on the rolling road with her son and two grandchildren. This cabin then included windows, a staircase and other improvements made after emancipation, but the fact that these old crude buildings, even with some improvements, were still being used as homes was a sign of the county's poverty.

Almost all those who had been born slaves at Sotterley had left by the late nineteenth century. "Uncle" Alfred Edwards was a rare exception. He had been born about 1847 a slave at Sotterley, the son of Lee Edwards, owned by Chapman Billingsley, and Priscilla Quentin, owned by Doctor Briscoe. He married Alice Kelly about 1882. In 1910 the census listed him as a "farmer" living with Alice and seven of their children and grandchildren in a former slave cabin across the ravine north of Sotterley on land that had belonged earlier to the Billingsleys. It is said that Nannie Williams too had been born a slave at Sotterley, but there is no evidence to substantiate it.

Alfred Edwards.

In these hard times, Sotterley declined markedly. The Cashners lived there during the warmer months, but economic circumstances forced them to rent part of the house year-round. The house was divided in such a way that the tenant family used the drawing room as their kitchen. By the dawn of the twentieth century, Sotterley was in danger of collapse, until good fortune in the person of Henry Yates Satterlee intervened to begin its rescue.

Satterlee was a descendant of the family that had owned Sotterley Hall in Suffolk until the fifteenth century. A New York native and graduate of Columbia University, he became an Episcopal priest and in the 1890s was serving as pastor of Calvary Church in New York. After turning down two other dioceses, Reverend Satterlee was appointed bishop of the new Diocese of Washington in 1896. He was a man of intellect and force, who is best known for overseeing the design and initial construction of the grand gothic National Cathedral in Washington.

Bishop Satterlee's diocese included southern Maryland. Although this worldly man is said to have taken relatively little interest in the rural part of his diocese, he did visit St. Andrew's Church and learned about Sotterley. Moreover, in 1891 he was one of a group of Satterlee descendants who had made the trip to Britain to visit their ancestral home, so he knew something of his family's history. (At that time Sotterley Hall was owned by the Barnes family, which had acquired it from the Platers in the eighteenth century.) Believing that Maryland's Sotterley was somehow closely linked to his own family's past, Bishop Satterlee was dismayed to see it had fallen into disrepair. Lacking resources of his own, the Bishop mentioned Sotterley to his second cousin, Herbert Livingston Satterlee, a wealthy lawyer in New York, and persuaded him to visit Sotterley.

On May 10, 1906, Herbert Satterlee and his wife, Louisa Pierpont Satterlee, the daughter of J. P. Morgan, and a Reverend Turner took the train from New York to Washington and caught the late afternoon steamboat for Leonardtown. They arrived the next morning, breakfasted at the Moore's Hotel, and took a carriage to Sotterley, where they were greeted by the Cashners. The party toured Sotterley and returned to Leonardtown that day in time to catch the night boat back to Washington. In a brief entry in her diary, Louisa described Sotterley as an "enchanting old place." The visit was enough to confirm Herbert Satterlee's interest. He asked the Cashners to inform him if ever they planned to sell it.

Bishop Henry Yates Satterlee.

In 1910, with Elizabeth Cashner in poor health and the family in need of money, Herbert Satterlee received a letter from the Cashners offering to sell Sotterley. He promptly accepted, and on July 30 of that year the purchase of just over four hundred acres was completed. Sotterley had new owners who could afford to restore it.

An enchanting old place.

The Chain of Rescue Connections

Sotterley in disrepair in 1910.

If George Plater I had chosen to emigrate to a different British colony,
his family would not have been living in Annapolis.

If George Plater II had married earlier, he would not have been available
to wed Rebecca.

If Rebecca had continued to have only girls, George III would not
have been born.

If George III had not renamed the property "Sotterley," our story would
have ended differently.

If the Briscoes had changed the property's name again, the name "Sotterley"
would have been lost.

If Henry Yates Satterlee had accepted assignment as Bishop in Minneapolis,
his diocese would not have included St. Mary's County.

If Bishop Satterlee had not been well educated, he might not have known of
his family's connection to Sotterley Hall in Suffolk.

If Bishop Satterlee had not had a very wealthy relative to contact, Herbert
Satterlee would not have visited.

If Herbert Satterlee had not been captivated, Sotterley would not have
been saved.

16

Colonial Revival

Herbert Satterlee was attracted to Sotterley by its connection to his family's origins in Suffolk, England, and for another reason as well. As the son-in-law of a powerful and famous man, Satterlee often lived in the shadow of J. P. Morgan. When, for example, the *New York Times* published an article on Sotterley in 1911, the headline read, "The Morgans and Plymouth Rock of the South." For Satterlee, the old farm was an interest he could pursue on his own and on behalf of the Satterlee family.

When he purchased it, he was not sure how the property had come to be named Sotterley and thought that perhaps some member of another branch of the Satterlee family had come to Maryland with its earliest settlers. But like Bishop Satterlee, he was convinced the home was linked in some way to his family, and that was why he bought it. He knew that the Platers had owned Sotterley for most of the eighteenth century, but only later did he learn that it was the Platers who had given Sotterley its name. Unfortunately, Bishop Satterlee had died in 1908 and hence could not see his interest in the property brought to fruition.

Herbert and Louisa Satterlee were also attracted by its considerable charm. They relished its "solitude" and thought of it as a place to which they could escape from their more hectic lives in New York. Some in St. Mary's County saw the arrival of the family of J. P. Morgan as an opportunity to realize the dream of a railway running the length of the county and linking it to the

Herbert Satterlee with dog.

markets in Washington and Baltimore, but Satterlee, who did not want his solitude disturbed, showed no interest in the project.

In addition to tranquility, Satterlee's other purpose in buying Sotterley was "to restore the buildings as they were about 1776, so as to show the manner in which a southern Maryland gentleman lived in those days." He did not rush into restoration—except for the roof and finding a place for a bathroom—because he wanted to study Maryland's colonial history and architecture. Otherwise the house was left as it was until 1915. His first important decision involved the roof and replacing its weathered shingles. In choosing to stain the new roof shingles red, he attempted to replicate the house's eighteenth-century style. The undersides of some remaining eighteenth-century shingles still show their original red color. Satterlee also had a new road built linking the end of Vista Road directly to Sotterley Wharf Road, along what is now the jib piece allee. His intent was to move wagon traffic to and from the wharf farther from the main house to preserve its quiet. In addition, he had several houses constructed for families who would manage the farm and do the restoration work.

The Satterlees continued to live in New York, travel frequently, and visit their other homes in New York, Connecticut, and Maine. Because he was only able to visit Sotterley a few times a year, he employed Charles Knott as farm manager. They communicated regularly by letter until phone service reached the Knotts' house in the 1920s. Earlier in 1915, when he was planning a longer stay at Sotterley, he told his mother, "In case you want to reach me in an emergency, get someone in New York to telephone Mr. L. M. Wise, the storekeeper at Hollywood to send me a message. His call is '35 ring six Mechanicsville, Maryland.'"

Over the next two decades, Satterlee purchased additional land that expanded the property to about one thousand acres. Most of his additional

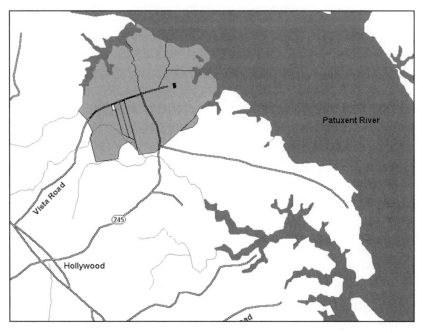

The Satterlees' property in 1947. Peter Himmelheber.

purchases were of land that in the nineteenth century had been owned by Colonel Billingsley. Bringing these thousand acres together in effect recreated the original 890 acres patented by James Bowles in 1716 and later called Sotterley by George Plater III.

On these visits, Satterlee, a formal and decorous man who was always referred to as "Mr. Satterlee" by those outside his family, reviewed the work that had been done and made plans for future projects. Occasionally, he enjoyed swims in Sotterley Creek, and Louisa exulted in the surroundings, particularly her roses in the garden. Often they were accompanied by daughters Mabel and Eleanor. Most of all, the Satterlees seemed to take pleasure in the quiet and natural beauty of Sotterley.

On longer stays, the family visited with their neighbors, the Cashners, the Thomas Bonds at Rosedale, and the Walter Briscoes on Half Pone. In June 1913, the Satterlees arrived on the late J. P. Morgan's yacht *Corsair III*, which the *St. Mary's Beacon* described as "a truly magnificent yacht, one of the finest now flying the American Flag." On Tuesday, June 10, the Satterlees invited neighbors and friends to a reception on board. The guest list included Mr. and Mrs. Thomas H. Bond, Mr. and Mrs. Walter H. S. Briscoe, Dr. and Mrs. A. L. Hodgdon, Mr. and Mrs. Frederic Taylor, Mrs. J. F. Lee Jr., Miss Eleanor Carroll, Mr. G. F. Wathen and Mr. John H. T. Briscoe. Both local papers reported this social occasion.

The Satterlees traveled to their new home, usually in the spring and fall, by means that reflected new developments in early twentieth-century transportation. Their initial trip was by steamboat from Washington to Leonardtown, then by carriage to Sotterley. Later they frequently took the steamboat from Baltimore and disembarked at Sotterley Wharf. In 1912 they rented an automobile in Washington and drove on the new paved "state" road to Leonardtown, from whence they rented carriages for the ride on the dirt road to Sotterley. At other times, they took the train to its terminus in Forrest Hall just south of Mechanicsville, where Charles Knott met them and drove them to the estate in a carriage. After World War I, a guest of the Satterlees once flew a seaplane to Sotterley and took their teenage daughter Mabel for a flight over the Patuxent. In the late 1920s, the family chauffer drove down from New York, picked them up at Washington's Union Station, and drove them on to St. Mary's, where their Rolls Royce attracted considerable attention.

After he had studied Maryland's history and agriculture for roughly five years, Herbert Satterlee began the process of transforming Sotterley. In 1915,

Louisa Satterlee with daughters Mabel and Eleanor.
Courtesy of Sandra van Heerden.

he and Louisa laid out plans for the kind of garden that might have been found at an eighteenth-century plantation. In 1915–16, they removed the Briscoes' two-story kitchen addition because it had not been part of the eighteenth-century house, and restored the piazza along the full length of the east side overlooking the Patuxent.

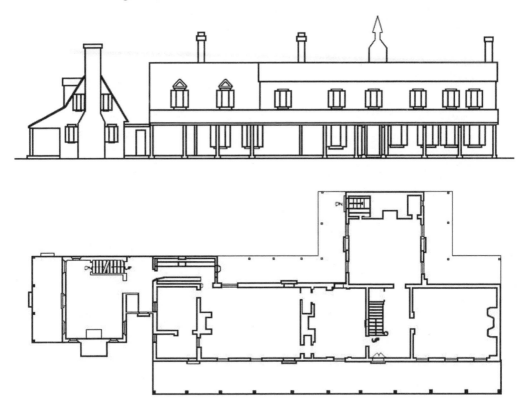

Front view of Satterlee house over floor plan.

Next they built a new two-story brick kitchen on the south end of the house, where they believed the kitchen might have been located in the Plater years. It was designed in a colonial revival style that blended well with the eighteenth-century house. Subsequently, they had the south gatehouse rebuilt together with a wrought-iron gate to create an attractive entry to the garden. In the 1920s, an allee of approximately seventy silver maples was planted leading from Vista Road to the garden entrance.

Satterlee provided the plans and financing, local craftsmen did the work, and Charles Knott oversaw the improvements while his wife, India, kept the accounts. James Mattingly built houses and did much of the fine carpentry. Louis Garner laid the brickwork in the gable ends of the mansion and for the new kitchen. John Wible did the wrought-iron work for the gates and cistern.

This restoration work was part of the wider colonial revival movement in the country, though Herbert Satterlee evidently made no reference to it by name. Around the time of the 1876 centennial of the Declaration of Independence, wealthy families began restoring eighteenth-century houses to mark their pride in the American Revolution and nostalgia for the colonial period. Although their work was based on research, the Satterlees did not try to restore the house exactly to what it had been in the eighteenth century, in part because it was also to be a vacation home for their family and friends. Rather, they appear to have had a romantic vision of how a charming eighteenth-century-style plantation could be recreated. Their vision resulted in beauty that continues to charm visitors a century later.

Improvements continued. Additional houses were built for the local craftsmen doing the construction. A horse barn was added in 1914 and a cow barn in 1916. A brick tool shed appeared in a corner of the garden, and a low brick wall was built along the north side of the garden between it and the "necessary." In the mid-thirties, extensive termite damage required that the house be lifted, dirt removed underneath, and a new cement foundation poured. Electricity reached Sotterley in 1939 and was installed first in the Knotts' house. In 1944 electricity was added to the first floor of the main house, except in the drawing room, which was to remain lit by candles as in the eighteenth century.

By the late 1920s, the house and grounds were in fine condition, and the Satterlees began to open the house not just to their invited guests but also to a variety of interested garden, veterans', and historical groups. One of the most ambitious events was "Plater Old Home Week," organized in May 1930. About forty Plater descendants returned for a pleasant reunion that attracted families from around the country.

Patuxent
St. Thomas Cre
Pasture
Upper field
Woods
Tenant house
Miss Lydia's house
Miss Lydia's field
Gate house
White Gate
Tenant houses
More or less field
Vista Road
Lodge
Spout Spring field
Farm house
Tobacco barn
Walters house
Forest
Stump field
Old Stump field
Oak Gate
Old Oak tree
School
Mill Run
Site of plaster mill
Road
N
W
E

Map of Sotterley in 1926 commissioned by Herbert Satterlee.

The 1930s saw one significant change. A hurricane in August 1933 destroyed Sotterley Wharf and many other wharves along the Patuxent. The wharf was not rebuilt. The age of steamboats and the one hundred years during which Sotterley's steamboat wharf had served as a local transportation hub had ended, replaced by the automobile and paved roads. The road from Leonardtown to Sotterley's gate had been paved in 1925. With the source of traffic removed, it became easier to preserve the Satterlees' solitude.

Occasionally, that solitude was interrupted. Early in World War II, the U.S. Navy opened the Patuxent Naval Air Station about fifteen miles south of Sotterley. One day in September 1943 the base's flight-testing program caused some unexpected excitement when a "Corsair" fighter undergoing flight testing made an emergency landing in Sotterley's fields and came to a stop just outside the brick wall by the garden. Pilot and property were unharmed.

In the late 1930s, Louisa's health began to decline and she was less able to travel. World War II broke out and brought with it gasoline rationing, so for a variety of reasons the family's visits to Sotterley became less frequent. Louisa Satterlee passed away in June 1946, and her husband, who had done so much for Sotterley, followed less than a year later.

Herbert and Louisa Satterlee

Herbert Livingston Satterlee (1863–1947) was a successful New York lawyer specializing in corporate and commercial law. He was a graduate of Columbia University where he received a law degree in 1885. During the Spanish-American War he served as a lieutenant in the navy and maintained a life-long interest in naval and maritime matters. In 1902, he took the lead in forming the Navy League, and in 1908–9 he served for three months as assistant secretary of the navy under President Theodore Roosevelt.

In 1900, Herbert married Louisa Pierpont Morgan (1865–1946), the eldest daughter of financier J. P. Morgan. Bishop Satterlee presided at a wedding that was the social event of the year in New York. The couple had two daughters, Mabel born in 1901, and Eleanor in 1905. Herbert and Louisa were involved in a host of New York social and philanthropic organizations.

Herbert Satterlee was also a writer, contributing to newspapers, magazines, and books as well as authoring a biography of his father-in-law, entitled *J. Pierpont Morgan: An Intimate Portrait, 1837–1912*. He also wrote the lyrics for several songs, including "Autumn Leaves," "Above the Shimmering Sea," and "When Arbutus Blooms in Southern Maryland."

Charles Knott.
Courtesy of Richard Knott.

17

Trustworthy Managers

W HEN HERBERT SATTERLEE agreed to buy Sotterley in 1910, he asked J. D Cashner to help find someone to manage the property. In those hard times, many came to apply for the position. Cashner chose Charles Knott, and the new proprietor subsequently confirmed the selection. From 1910 until 1993, Charles Knott and his sons were the careful stewards of Sotterley for Satterlee and later for his daughter Mabel Ingalls, both of whom were visionary, strong-willed, and demanding owners. That their trust and satisfaction with the estate's management continued through eight decades is a tribute to the Knotts' character and ability.

Charles Knott was born in 1884 at Buzzards Point on Breton Bay. He had roughly five years of education and during 1908–9 had been working on a police boat. In 1910 he was just twenty-six years old and living on nearby Rosedale Farm. One night, he walked to Sotterley so that he might apply for the job as farm manager the next morning. He was chosen despite his youth and limited experience and despite competition from several others. On one of his first visits, Satterlee saw Knott working in the fields and called him to a meeting to explain that he should act like a manager. His job was to supervise, not do farm work himself. Satterlee told him to wear a suit and tie in the winter and white pants and shirt in the summer. The two men always addressed one another as "Mr. Satterlee" and "Mr. Knott." Everyone at Sotterley addressed them the same way.

One of the first things Satterlee did after acquiring the farm was to build a house for Charles Knott at the top of Sotterley Wharf Road. In 1912, Charles met India Leola Bond, also of St. Mary's County. They were married in 1913 and together had five children: Herbert, Margaret, Edward, Richard, and John, the last of whom died in childbirth. This was the family that played a central role at Sotterley for more than eighty years.

The Satterlees visited Sotterley two or three times a year, typically in the spring and fall, staying for several days each time. Mabel Ingalls visited frequently during World War II, when she was working in Washington, but later also adopted a pattern of visiting three or four times a year, typically for up to a week at a time. As a result, Charles Knott, and later Edward and Richard, bore the heavy responsibility of managing Sotterley during their absences. Knott had to oversee restoration work, supervise a variety of contractors, hire staff to work in the main house and garden, prepare for the Satterlees' visits, and manage a thousand-acre farm. Sotterley was the only one of Herbert Satterlee's properties that included a working farm, but he left it to his manager to decide on crops, choose livestock, supervise the tenant farmers, hire workers, and prepare items for shipment to the Satterlees or sale.

"Mr. Satterlee" and "Mr. Knott" maintained a weekly correspondence on all these matters. As Charles Knott had had only a few years of formal education, it was his practice to dictate letters to his wife India, who had a reputation for perfect spelling.

Herbert Satterlee was quite solicitous of the needs of those working at Sotterley. After building the house for the Knotts, he had houses built for several others. In 1911 a house was built for James Mattingly, who did the construction on these homes and subsequently on the new brick kitchen. "Wharf House" was built for Noah Callis the wharf tender at Sotterley Wharf; it is now owned by the van Heerdens, Mabel Ingalls's daughter and granddaughter. In 1913, Brink Cottage was built for Edward Knott, Charles's brother. Subsequently, Satterlee had homes built for James Scriber and Walter Barber so that their families could move out of the former slave cabins in which they had been living.

In the Satterlee era, wheat, corn, and some tobacco were the principal crops, along with barley, oats, and hay. In the early years, farming was done with horses. Beginning in the 1920s, Satterlee bought tractors and threshing machines for use at Sotterley and on neighboring farms. Livestock became a core business. Sotterley raised hogs and cattle for their meat, sheep for wool

India Knott. From Richard Knott, "Memories."

and meat, chickens for eggs, and turkeys. In the 1920s and 1930s the farm had about fifty hogs, sixty cattle, a hundred sheep, two hundred turkeys and seventy-five chickens. The hogs were slaughtered at Sotterley to make smoked ham and sausage; cattle and sheep were sold. Some of the produce was processed and shipped to the Satterlees and their friends in New York for Christmas. The Satterlees were particularly fond of turkeys and sausage made by the Knotts, and of preserves prepared by India Knott. The Knotts, Scribers, and other families had milk cows. In addition, there were workhorses for the farm and riding horses for Mabel.

The depression that wracked the nation in the 1930s had little impact on Sotterley. Thanks to Herbert Satterlee's resources and concern, all those working there kept their jobs and continued to receive salaries and benefits. Charles Knott even found part-time work for others in the local community. Despite a serious drought in 1930, Sotterley came through the Depression relatively unscathed.

Charles Knott respected Herbert Satterlee, loved Sotterley, and was proud of his accomplishments there. He conveyed that love to his children. Mabel Ingalls recalled that the Knotts almost worshiped her father. Satterlee in turn trusted Knott and appreciated his work and service. These two very different men shared a common love for the farm. When Herbert Satterlee died, Knott received what his family considered to be a generous bequest.

After Satterlee's death in 1947, Mabel Ingalls decided to buy Sotterley from her father's estate. In 1949 she wrote to Knott to say, "I would not have dared take on the responsibility unless I had felt sure that you and Mrs. Knott would stay on." Knott did, continuing to manage Sotterley for another ten years. After forty-eight years of service he moved to live on his son Richard's farm in Hollywood. Thereafter, his son Edward took over his responsibilities and continued to live with his family in the Knott House at Sotterley. Charles Knott passed away in 1970, and India in 1975.

Mabel Ingalls changed Sotterley by opening the house to the public, establishing the Sotterley Mansion Foundation, and gradually selling farmland that was not to be part of the foundation. To accommodate these changes, she gave Edward Knott responsibility for the foundation's property and in 1971 asked Richard Knott to return to Sotterley to manage farm operations. With less land, farm operations were reduced during the late 1970s and 1980s. Wheat, corn, and soybeans were the principal crops. Over time the farm's livestock operation was limited to raising sheep.

Richard Knott had been born at Sotterley in 1925 and held many fond memories of growing up there and learning to hunt, fish, and crab along with his brothers. He had attended elementary and middle school at St. John's Church's parochial school and had worked at Sotterley as a boy earning ten cents and hour. He remembers fondly the men working on the farm when he was young and credits his father and those men with teaching him the meaning of "an honest day's work." Between 1943 and 1971, Richard had managed an oyster marketing business and with his wife Virginia lived on Forest Landing Farm in Hollywood. While running his business, he had also assisted his father with work at Sotterley, so it was quite natural that he agreed to her request.

Richard Knott developed a close relationship with Mabel Ingalls, who trusted him to "take care of her farm," and he expressed his deep respect for her in loyalty and service. He particularly remembers that she was willing to support him in difficult circumstances provided she believed he was right. In the last years of Mabel Ingalls's life, he and Edward Knott's son Donald were still working at Sotterley.

Like his father, Richard is proud of his family's contribution to Sotterley. In 2003 he and his grandson Shawn Knott authored "Memories of Sotterley" as a reflection of his love for the place. After the Knotts' decades of dedicated service, Sotterley owes them a debt of gratitude.

Edward Knott.
Courtesy of Richard Knott.

Richard Knott.
Courtesy of Richard Knott.

James Scriber.

18

Tenants and Workers

WELL BEFORE 1900, Dr. Briscoe had passed on, and the Kanes and most former slaves had moved to begin new lives elsewhere. Slavery was history, but segregation persisted. In the first half of the twentieth century, new segregation and miscegenation laws strengthened the legal separation of blacks and whites in Maryland. The black population of St. Mary's County declined from 8,256 in 1900 to 4,724 in 1940. Many joined the great migration of southern blacks to northern cities, with most from St. Mary's County moving to Baltimore. Agnes Kane Callum's father Philip Morton Kane moved there in 1917, married Priscilla Gough, and stayed to find work in the city. Many others in the extended Kane family also moved to Baltimore and Washington in this period.

Around 1910, when the Satterlees became the new owners, several black families were at Sotterley. Two who were living there as tenants to the Cashners remained and played important roles at Sotterley in the new century. They were the families of James Scriber and Walter Barber.

James Victor Scriber was born on March 17, 1878, in Hollywood. His father, James, had come from Georgia. His mother, Anna Smallwood, was the descendant of slaves from Calvert County. When James was six, his family left Hollywood and moved to Sotterley, where they lived in a one-room former slave cabin. James's father had worked on steamboats. The family's living standard was "very, very low," and at times there was not enough to eat. Schools were not available for black children then, and James never learned to read and write. Once grown, he went to New Jersey to work as a farm hand, but he returned to Sotterley and in 1906 married Nettie Lyles. They lived in a former slave cabin near the top of Sotterley Wharf Road, working as tenants first for the Cashners, then as tenant farmers working for the Satterlees.

James and Nettie had sixteen children, all born at home with the help of midwives. The first five arrived while the couple lived in the former slave cabin. In 1917, Herbert Satterlee had a house built for James's growing family across the field to the north of Sotterley's garden. The other children, including daughter Nettie, were born in this new home. James was a sharecropper, meaning that when the crops were sold the income was split between James, the tenant, and Herbert Satterlee, the owner. The Satterlees provided the land, seed, fertilizer, draught animals, farm equipment, and a house. James and his sons provided the labor. James had about fifteen acres in corn, fifteen in wheat, and four in tobacco, with the crops rotated and other grains and hay grown as needed. In his spare time, he also worked on the garden and grounds around the main house. The Scribers had milk cows, hogs, chickens, and a garden of their own. Sharecropping was hard work. The sons worked from the time they were seven or eight weeding the corn and tobacco with hoes.

In the 1920s and 1930s, the Scriber and Knott children grew up together. James Scriber's daughter Nettie fondly remembers playing with Richard Knott, crabbing in the summer, sledding in the winter, fishing, hunting possum, and racing to meet arriving steamboats at Sotterley Wharf. She recalls that "color was no problem" at Sotterley. Relations among the several families living there were friendly. "There was no strife." The Knott and Scriber boys called each other by nicknames. Richard Knott was known as "Sharpy."

In those years, most of the skilled craftsmen hired to do construction and renovation were white, while of those hired to do farm work and housekeeping were black. The Knott men and boys, other than Charles, performed a wide range of tasks including farming. Richard remembers his older brothers, uncles, and himself sharing farm work with James Scriber. The Satterlees employed Nettie Scriber and Harriet Barber as cooks and housekeepers in the main house. They prepared favorite meals for the Satterlees, served the food, cleaned the house, did the laundry, repaired linens, and canned preserves to be shipped to the Satterlees in New York. Over the years a succession of Scriber and Barber women worked in the main house.

In December 1935, James's wife Nettie Scriber died. Their daughter Nettie, then fourteen years old, left school to be at home looking after her younger siblings. Three years later, James married Laura Coats. After his sons had grown and left home, James was no longer able to continue sharecropping on his own, for their labor had been essential to his sharecropping. Around 1943, when the Patuxent River Naval Air Station was being built, James took a construction job on the base.

Philip Scriber was born at Sotterley in 1928, the second youngest of James and Nettie Scriber's children. As a young boy he, like some of his siblings, went to the Phyllis Wheatley School, a two-room elementary and secondary school for blacks about three and a half miles away on Sotterley Road. He recalls that white children were bused, but black children had to walk. Philip only went to school for a couple of years before beginning work in the fields when he was about eight. He never considered sharecropping himself, because he thought the work too hard and the system "unfair." Nevertheless, he and his sister Nettie both said that "Mr. Satterlee" had been "generous" to their family. Other people were envious of those working at Sotterley because their wages were higher.

Philip recalls that whites called older blacks "uncle" and "aunt" as their way of showing a measure of respect, but he also noted that they did not refer to himself or his wife as "Mr." and "Mrs." Philip also recalls that his father had always farmed in the traditional way. Although Herbert Satterlee bought tractors beginning in the 1920s, James Scriber never used them, for he was reluctant to adopt new ways. Philip said that his father later regretted that he had paid too much attention to what white people told him.

Daughter Nettie Scriber married Joseph Ignatius Stevens and moved to his home in Hollywood, where he worked on the Thompson farm. Nettie was a laundress, though she continued to work at Sotterley and often came in the evenings to serve meals when Mabel

Nettie Scriber Stevens.
Courtesy of Richard Knott.

Ingalls was there. Nettie worked in the main house almost all her life. In 1997, Sotterley's board of trustees presented her with a certificate of appreciation for her many years of devoted service and her loving care.

The other long-time family were the Barbers. Walter Barber was born in 1872, the son of John and Caroline Barber who were living in Hillville in 1880. Where this Barber family lived before 1880 is unknown, but it is believed that they came from Upper Marlboro in Prince Georges County. Around 1901,

Walter Barber.

Walter married Harriet Dyson. When the Cashners owned Sotterley, Walter and Harriet were tenants living in a former slave cabin located near the Black Gate. The Black Gate, on Sotterley Road at the intersection with Steer Horn Neck Road, was the entrance to Sotterley until the 1960s. The Barbers stayed on as employees for the Satterlees. Walter was responsible for livestock, tending horses, cows, and sheep. Harriet worked in the main house as a cook and housekeeper. In 1917, Herbert Satterlee had a new house built for the Barbers on what is now Tranquility Lane. Walter and Harriet had seven children, including sons Ford and Bernard. All were born at Sotterley. Richard Knott recalls that Walter was very much dedicated to the farm.

Bernard and Ford Barber worked at Sotterley as children. They too attended the Phyllis Wheatley School, Bernard for six years. Ford attended somewhat longer and eventually became a mechanic at Sotterley responsible for maintaining the farm equipment. Bernard moved away as a young man to work elsewhere but returned to St. Mary's County and in 1934 married Ruth Somerville. Together they raised seven children at Sotterley. Bernard and Ruth lived in various houses on the land owned by Herbert Satterlee. Their daughter Phyllis was born in 1945. Around 1950, Bernard's family moved into the house in which James Scriber's family had lived earlier. Bernard worked as a farm hand for many years and took care of Sotterley's garden and grounds. He also did light carpentry, plumbing, and some mechanical work. Ruth worked as a housekeeper and cook in the main house. The times were hard but Bernard and Ruth were strong, resilient people.

Phyllis Barber remembers living a quiet family-centered life as a child in the 1950s in the "secluded" farm setting. At that time, there were no other children near her age in the neighborhood. Her mother, Ruth, had attended Cardinal Gibbons School for nine years and read to her children and encouraged their education. Phyllis was not conscious of segregation—that was something encountered when one left Sotterley. Restaurants and bars were segregated. The Barbers frequented the ABC Snack Bar, a bar for blacks in Hollywood at the intersection of Sotterley and Old Three Notch Roads. Movie theaters had a separate entrance for blacks, who sat in the balcony. Before she was six and eligible for school, Phyllis was in the habit of accompanying her older brothers to the Phyllis Wheatley School. At that time, kindergarten was not provided for black children. Later, Phyllis attended the Banneker School for blacks in Loveville, which had classes from first to twelfth grades but no kindergarten program. In the 1950s and 1960s, black children were bused to Banneker. The school was not fully integrated until 1967 after she had graduated. Her brothers, Gerard and Donald, began at Banneker but moved to their neighborhood school, the integrated Hollywood Elementary School, in 1965. For young Phyllis, segregation was not an issue; it was just "the way things were." With a nurturing family at home and friends at school, she enjoyed a happy childhood.

Bernard and Ruth worked first for Herbert Satterlee and subsequently for Mabel Ingalls. Their relationship was one of employer and employee, but Bernard and Ruth got along well with the owners. They too thought Herbert Satterlee was a very generous man. Each time a child was born, he had a layette sent from Macy's, whose main store was on New York's Fifth Avenue not far from the Satterlee residence. At Christmas the children, like the others living at Sotterley, each received a present. Bernard died in 1971. He and Ruth were remembered as people who were "loyal, honest and dependable" and committed to Sotterley.

Phyllis at times accompanied her mother when she was working in the main house, and there she met Mabel Ingalls, whom she remembers as a woman of strong will who knew what she wanted. Phyllis must have made an impression because, before she had graduated from high school, Mabel asked her to become one of the early tour guides showing visitors around Sotterley. The experience gave her a deeper understanding of Sotterley's history and sparked a lifelong interest in fine furniture and furnishings. When Phyllis graduated from Banneker, Mabel sent a note and gift. This kindness was repeated when Phyllis graduated from college and again when she completed graduate school. In fact, Mabel Ingalls sent a small monetary gift and card to each Barber child when they graduated from high school and another for their college graduation. Upon receipt of each gift, Ruth insisted that her children immediately respond with a handwritten thank-you note. In later years, Mabel invited Ruth to have lunch with her.

The Scribers and Barbers were Catholic. Both families attended St. John's Church in Hollywood, the same church the Knotts attended. Nettie Scriber remembers walking to St. John's every Sunday in the 1930s and enjoying the opportunity to socialize with neighbors and friends at church. Bernard and Ruth were married at St. John's. Phyllis Barber remembers enjoying the annual summer festivals at the church, where she too married her husband, James Brown. St. John's was partially integrated, and the congregation attended services together, though whites sat in front and blacks in the pews at the

Bernard and Ruth Barber with son Bernard Jr.
Courtesy of Donald Barber.

back. St. John's operated a parochial school, but it was only for white children. The priests and nuns were white.

In 1974, Ruth Barber married her second husband, James Edward Scriber, a son of the elder James Scriber, and the family moved to her new husband's home in Hollywood. Ruth continued to work at Sotterley generally three days a week, keeping the main house in pristine condition, cleaning, polishing silver, and doing needlework repairs on the fine linens.

The establishment of the Patuxent Naval Air Station during World War II brought change to St. Mary's County. The base and the war created new opportunities for those living at Sotterley. Pax River was one of the few places where blacks could find jobs that paid enough to support a family. In 1943, James Scriber took a construction job there, and by 1946 he had saved enough to buy a forty-nine-acre property nearby.

The growth brought by Pax River and the expanding educational opportunities made it possible for St. Mary's County to share in the nation's post-war prosperity. In 1944, Philip Scriber got a job at Pax River by pretending to be eighteen and was subsequently drafted. During his years in the military, he took advantage of opportunities to get an education. Ruth Barber's second husband James also worked at the base and was able to buy what became Scriber's Bar in Leonardtown. Phyllis Barber Brown went to college and graduate school and pursued a career in education, specializing in reading. Gerard and Donald Barber also went to college. The Barber family's commitment to Sotterley continues through Donald's service as trustee and treasurer of Historic Sotterley Inc.

There were of course many others who were employed at Sotterley during the twentieth century, but the Scribers and Barbers stand out for their long and dedicated service and their contributions to maintaining the house and its grounds for all those who come to enjoy Sotterley's beauty.

19

Creating a Foundation
for the Future

MABEL SATTERLEE INGALLS, the eldest of Herbert and Louisa Satterlee's children, was the last owner of Sotterley. She had visited from the time she was a teenager and remembered her time there fondly. Her father had sent several horses to Sotterley so that she could go riding with the friends. When she was older, she and her husband hunted quail together. During World War II when she was working at Walter Reed Army Medical Center, she made frequent visits with her daughter Sandra.

When Herbert Satterlee died, his will stipulated that all of his properties, including Sotterley, were to be sold. Given his love of the place, it is hard to believe that he had not made some arrangement to preserve his considerable emotional and financial investment in it. Mabel loved and admired her father and understood its importance to him. After giving the matter some thought, she decided to buy Sotterley. It was the only one of her parents' properties that she did purchase. Just when her decision crystallized is not clear, but in July 1948, when the purchase was being arranged, she wrote: "I do not want to own a large farm in Maryland and my idea is to sell most of the acreage. . . . I want to keep the mansion, the old brick barn and about 100 acres." In October 1948 she purchased the one-thousand-acre property from the Satterlee estate for $120,000. Charles Knott remained as manager. Around 1950, she built a

A youthful Mabel Ingalls. Courtesy of Sandra van Heerden.

new home for the Knotts within easy view of the main house. That house is now the Sotterley office. Charles's son, Edward, and his family took over the Knott house as their home.

Mabel Ingalls did not change the architecture of the main house, but she greatly influenced its decoration and furnishings. She had studied

Abbott, Mabel and Sandra Ingalls c. 1940. Courtesy of Sandra van Heerden.

watercolor painting and had a special appreciation for color. Her father had painted all the downstairs rooms in antique white. Mabel chose new colors, including the bold red for Madame Bowles's Chamber and a pale yellow for the drawing room. She had seen a palm tree motif wallpaper on a visit to Brighton Pavilion in England and approached Phelps Warren, owner of a wallpaper firm in New York that specialized in historic homes. Warren found the pattern, and Mabel chose a shade of that paper for the dining room. On a visit to Hong Kong, she had a rug woven for the dining room using the same color scheme as the wallpaper.

Mrs. Ingalls believed that more could be done to take advantage of Sotterley as an historic home, and she gradually developed plans to encourage public interest in it. One step was to include the house and its gardens on various home tours arranged by garden clubs and historic associations. That led to a relationship with the Society for the Preservation of Maryland Antiquities (SPMA), a predecessor to today's Maryland Historic Trust. In the 1950s, Sotterley was opened to the public on a more regular basis under the auspices of the SPMA.

The next step was to form a nonprofit foundation. Mabel Ingalls credited Robert Thrun, her lawyer, with explaining how this could be accomplished, and on April 25, 1960, the Sotterley Mansion Foundation was established in New York. She and her daughter Sandra van Heerden, together with Robert Thrun and Mabel's friend Phelps Warren, were the original trustees. In 1962 she transferred the first donation of land, including the main house, gardens, allee, and rolling road, to the foundation. She also hired its first employee, Sue Milton, to serve as resident docent and administrator. Looking back years later, Mrs. Ingalls said that her purpose in creating the foundation was "to show how people had lived here and farmed the land all this time since about 1717." While her father's initial goal had been to restore the house to show how a gentleman had lived in 1776, he and Mabel both came to see that Sotterley was important as a wider window into history from the early eighteenth to the late twentieth century.

The decision to establish the foundation was part of a new national interest in historic preservation. The SPMA had been created in 1931. The nonprofit National Trust for Historic Preservation was established thirty years later. Also in 1961, information on Sotterley was submitted to the Department of the Interior for inclusion in their Historic American Buildings Survey. In 1972, Sotterley was included in the National Park Service's newly established National Register of Historic Places.

But for Mabel Ingalls, Sotterley was more than a philanthropic interest. She loved her regular visits in the spring and autumn, and she surrounded herself with friends whom she sought to interest in it. She converted several houses that her father had built on the property into homes she rented to friends from New York and Washington, including Molly Thayer, Gordon and Carolyn Williams, and Grace and John Horton. In the early 1950s she moved the spinning cottage to the lawn overlooking the river and used it as a place other friends could rent for short-term visits. In the 1960s she gave annual Memorial Day weekend house parties to which she invited friends from Washington, New York, and Maryland. Her guests remember a convivial hostess serving whiskey sours and soft crabs on the piazza, along with country ham, biscuits, and strawberries, all from Sotterley.

One of her most prestigious guests was Crown Prince Harald of Norway. For forty years, Mabel spent several weeks each summer in Norway. She was part-owner of a twelve-meter sailboat there and enjoyed sailing and fishing along the coast. When in 1960 she learned that the Crown Prince would be on a tour of the U.S., she invited him to visit Sotterley.

By 1970 she had separated the management of the foundation and its property from the farm. Edward Knott handled the grounds and buildings of the foundation, and Richard Knott managed the farm. In addition, the foundation employed a series of residents to serve as administrator and docent. The most dedicated of these was Elizabeth Harman, who filled this role from 1969 to 1982 as an employee and thereafter continued for another fifteen years as an active volunteer docent. With Sotterley's main house regularly open to the public, it became increasingly awkward for Mabel to use it as her own residence. (At times visitors were escorted through the dining room while she was having a late breakfast—a treat for the visitors if not always for her.) Consequently in the early 1980s, Mabel stopped living in the main house. By 1988 she completed a renovation of Wharf House and resided there during her visits.

In planning the foundation's future, Mabel Ingalls gradually implemented her desire to sell off land that would not become part of the foundation. She was greatly concerned that real estate development not affect Sotterley. After the opening of the Patuxent Naval Air Station in 1942, St. Mary's County began to change. From 1890 until 1940 its population had remained at about 15,000, but between 1940 and 1990 that figure grew to 75,000. As development became a serious threat to Sotterley, she sought to sell land to people she knew and to write usage restrictions into the sales documents. Her goal was to protect the appearance of the approach into Sotterley and all land that could be seen from the main house. This included the land down to Sotterley Creek and the fields on Sotterley Point. To date, her efforts have been remarkably successful.

Mabel Ingalls catches a Norwegian Salmon, Eirefjord, Norway, 1949.
Courtesy of Sandra van Heerden.

The original trustees were all from New York. In expanding the board during its first decade, Mabel brought in people from Washington and elsewhere who were specialists in historic homes as well as a few prominent figures from St. Mary's County. The first two county members were Spence Howard and Charles Fenwick. Nevertheless, in the 1970s board members were still primarily from outside southern Maryland. In seeking advice from John Hanson Briscoe and others, she learned that county people did not always feel welcome at Sotterley, so in 1977 the trustees invited some residents of southern Maryland to join a council to advise the board. Richard Plater, a descendant of the Plater family living in Virginia, also joined the council. In the 1980s more local leaders, including J. Frank Raley, Hope Swann, and John Hanson Briscoe were recruited to join the board.

Mabel Ingalls continued to visit Sotterley throughout her life. She was particularly interested in the garden, picturing it and the grounds as the frame around the charming main house. Late in life she kept a set of gardening clothes in the closet and at times was seen by visitors working in the garden.

She was also eager to develop Sotterley's cultural and educational possibilities. In the 1980s, Marianne Chapman and Hope Swann from the St. Mary's County Education Department developed a series of educational programs run by the county at Sotterley. Mabel asked Grace Horton to join the board and organize musical programs. She met Agnes Kane Callum when Agnes brought a group of children and relatives from Baltimore for a program on slavery. She welcomed Agnes's research and saw the new educational ways in which Sotterley could be used. In 1990 the county commissioners presented her with a plaque commending her support for education. The plaque now hangs on the west wall of the main house.

Mabel Ingalls had kept tight control over Sotterley and the foundation as was appropriate, since she was the owner as well as the creator and financer of the foundation. However, in 1990 at age eighty-nine she stepped back to become president emeritus, and Sandra van Heerden assumed the duties of president. As these changes were being made, the board adopted a new statement that the foundation's mission henceforth would be "to educate culturally, aesthetically and historically the public and students, particularly as to the basis of the rights of man, the basis of our democratic process and the basis of our ideals and institutions."

Sandra, who like her mother spent most of her time in New York, soon recognized that the foundation needed a president who was resident in St. Mary's. In 1992 she asked John Hanson Briscoe to take on the responsibility. His acceptance marked the shift from family to local leadership of the foundation.

In 1993, Mabel Ingalls died. Her passing marked the end of both the eighty-year Satterlee era and the nearly three centuries in which Sotterley had been a private residence owned by a succession of families. The foundation assumed the new responsibility of operating Sotterley as a nonprofit historic home, but the family's role in Sotterley continued. Mabel Ingalls had established a family fund that continued to provide partial financial support. Sandra transferred additional property to the foundation, and she and her daughter have remained actively involved in its affairs.

Mabel Ingalls. Courtesy of Sandra van Heerden.

Mabel Satterlee Ingalls

MABEL INGALLS was born August 13, 1901, in Great Neck, New York. She was the eldest daughter of Herbert and Louisa Satterlee and married Francis Abbott Ingalls in 1926. Their only child, Sandra, was born in 1932. The marriage ended in divorce in 1947.

After graduating from the Brearely School in New York in 1918, she earned a bachelor of science degree from Barnard College in 1925, a master's degree from Radcliffe (Harvard Medical School) in 1928, a doctorate from Columbia University in 1937, and a master's degree in public health from Columbia in 1954.

From 1936 to 1943 she taught in the Department of Pathology and Bacteriology at the Albany Medical School. During World War II she conducted medical research at the Walter Reed Medical Center in Washington. In 1945–46, she served with the United Nations Relief and Rehabilitation Agency in Europe, and from 1949 to 1957 served as a liaison officer between the U.N. and the World Health Organization. From 1958 until her retirement in 1964, Mabel was an adjunct associate professor at Columbia University's School of Public Health.

In retirement, Mabel Ingalls was associated for many years with International Social Service, a non-governmental organization headquartered in Geneva, and with the Community Development Trust Fund of Tanzania. She had a life-long interest in family planning and worked with the Margaret Sanger Research Bureau of Planned Parenthood in New York.

Mabel Ingalls lived a full, rich life with a wide variety of interests. As a young woman she conducted research in British Guyana. She also worked as a freelance reporter in the Balkans. An avid outdoorswoman, she enjoyed riding, sailing and fishing and was an early member of the Women's Fly-fishers Club. She loved racing International One Design sailboats from her home at Northeast Harbor, Maine.

20

Sotterley Today

Historic Sotterley, Inc., the successor to the Sotterley Mansion Foundation, is a nonprofit educational organization that serves the community and is sustained by active community involvement and support. Historic Sotterley manages about ninety acres. The property encompasses some two dozen original buildings spanning three centuries, about half of which are located in the historic preservation core area, which includes most importantly the main house and the slave cabin. After being on the brink of closing in the late 1990s, Sotterley has become an integral part of the cultural landscape of St. Mary's County. In recognition of its importance as a cultural resource, the Department of the Interior designated Sotterley as a National Historic Landmark in 2000.

The Mission of Historic Sotterley, Inc., is to preserve, research and interpret Sotterley Plantation's diverse cultures and environments and to serve as a public educational resource.

The board of trustees and staff see this mission as a public trust to be pursued for the benefit of the community. Sotterley endeavors to accomplish its mission in several ways:

— By using Sotterley as a site for cultural and community programs,

— Through the excellence of its educational programs,

— Through a variety of accessible, quality interpretative offerings,

— By careful stewardship of the buildings and environment, and

— Through continuing research on Sotterley's history and relevance.

Sotterley conducts educational programs of its own and also acts as a host site for two of St. Mary's County's environmental education programs. The hands-on education programs offered by Sotterley are: "Colonial Tidewater Plantation Life," "RiverWays," "Dig This: An Archaeological Field Day," and the award-winning "Slavery to Freedom." All education programs can be adapted for different grade levels or customized for special interest. Sotterley's programs meet the Maryland Voluntary State Curriculum Standards for social studies and are routinely recognized by the state for their excellent content and execution.

Throughout its history, Sotterley has always thrived by virtue of the efforts of those who lived there. Today, Sotterley's people are its members, about 180 volunteers from the community, a dedicated staff, and a volunteer board of trustees. The board includes leaders with backgrounds in historic preservation, education, museum management, horticulture, construction, and, of course, finance and marketing. Descendants of the Satterlee, Briscoe, Kane, and Barber families are actively involved, working together to preserve their families' histories. With the hard work and dedication of all of those committed to the mission and preservation of Sotterley, this national treasure will remain a part of our shared history and legacy for many years to come.

FURTHER READING

The articles are arranged in chronological order as a reminder to readers that each article reflects what was known at the time it was written.

"The Morgans and Plymouth Rock of the South," *New York Times*, March 12, 1911.

McHenry Howard, "Three Platers," *Maryland Historical Magazine* 15 (1920): 168–80.

Herbert L. Satterlee, "Sotterley: The Southern Maryland Home on the Patuxent River of the Platers and the Briscoes." Unpublished manuscript, 1926. Available at Sotterley.

Marian McKenna, "Sotterley, St. Mary's County," *Maryland Historical Magazine* 46 (1951): 173–88.

[Mabel Ingalls and the Sotterley Trustees], *Sotterley, St. Mary's County, Maryland.* Printed for the Sotterley Mansion Foundation [1965]. Available at Sotterley.

Joan Boker, "A Visit to Sotterley," *Chesapeake Country Life*, vol. 2, no. 1, May–June 1981. Available at Sotterley.

Jennifer Keisman, "The Platers and Sotterley," *Chronicles of St. Mary's* 43 (Winter 1995): 81–91.

Peter Himmelheber, "The Resurrection Manner of the Resurrection Manor," *Chronicles of St. Mary's* 46 (Spring 1998): 275–80.

Kirk E. Ranzetta, "Sotterley Plantation: A Chronological Timeline." Prepared for the Sotterley Foundation, October 1998. Available at Sotterley.

Page T. Faust, "Keeping History Alive at Sotterley Plantation," *Chronicles of St. Mary's* 46 (Winter 1998): 338–42.

Richard Knott and Shawn Knott, *Memories of Sotterley* (n.p.: The authors, 2003).

Peter Himmelheber, "Sotterley Plantation During the War of 1812," *Chronicles of St. Mary's* 51 (Winter 2003): 90–93.

David G. Brown, "Getting Ahead in Colonial Maryland," *Chronicles of St. Mary's* 54 (Spring 2007): 401–7.

———, "George Plater and Maryland's First Constitution," *Chronicles of St. Mary's* 55 (Fall 2008): 547–53.

———, "George Plater: Patriot for Independence," *Maryland Historical Magazine* 104 (2009): 52–65.

INDEX

References to illustrations appear in italics